ERIE

UNDER

GOULD AND FISK.

A COMPARISON OF THE PAST AND PRESENT MANAGEMENT,
RESPECTFULLY DEDICATED TO THE STOCKHOLDERS
AND BONDHOLDERS GENERALLY.

BY GEORGE CROUCH.

NEW YORK.

1870.

PREFACE.

THE facts contained in the pamphlet entitled "Another Chapter of Erie" were first submitted to the public in the columns of the New York *World*, of December 11, 1869, under the then novel and somewhat startling caption, "A Plea for Erie." The article attracted the attention of the press throughout the country, many influential journals finding it of sufficient public interest to be reproduced *in extenso;* and in financial circles and the railroad world, its favorable exhibit of the results accomplished by the able management of Gould and Fisk, occasioned no little surprise. Those who had been most influenced by the unfavorable reports so industriously circulated by baffled monopolists and speculators, confidently predicted the speedy publication of such an irresistible counterblast of contradictions as should materially damage, if not completely demolish the writer's reputation for veracity, and at the same time close the public ear to any further pleas for Erie. But the members of the different cliques in league against President Gould and his official associates were thoroughly aware of the satisfactory condition of the road and its business while they were fabricating and promulgating their infamous reports to the contrary, and they, of all men, knew whether the statements published in the *World* were reliable or not, and therefore, made no attempt to challenge them. Let them forever after hold their peace.

Such general interest being manifested in the affairs of Erie, the writer was induced to republish the result of his investigations in pamphlet form. An edition of 10,000 copies of the Second Chapter, which was disposed of in the course of a few weeks, having failed to satisfy public curiosity, the present extension—a brief history of Erie under Gould and Fisk is respectfully submitted.

G. C.

New York, *March*, 1870.

ERIE UNDER GOULD AND FISK.

AUDI ALTERAM PARTEM.

Messrs. Gould and Fisk need put forward no other defence than the history of the Erie road under their management. It effectually silences all the malicious statements which have been so industriously circulated in the interest of rival parties and corporations for the purpose of injuring them in the estimation of the general public, and destroying the confidence of such as are pecuniarily interested in the magnificent property entrusted to their care, and proves them fully entitled to the commendation, "Well done, thou good and faithful servants." Aware of the fact that a very considerable quantity of the figurative dirt with which the reputations of these men have been so profusely bespattered acquired adhesive properties in consequence of the utter contempt with which those who hurled it were regarded; and that—in spite of all that has been done since Gould and Fisk were at length roused to self-defence, in order to preserve the credit of the corporation—so much yet sticks, the writer confidently anticipates seeing the above commendation of the two best-abused men in the world characterized as "sublimely audacious," or something equally complimentary. With equal confidence, however, does he rely upon the final verdict of public opinion. As the matter stands now, with such powerful prejudices to fight against, whoever undertakes to defend Fisk and Gould on any one of the counts of the voluminous indictment prepared by their persecutors must be equally ready to defend himself: in proof of which the following case may be cited. On the publication of Jay Gould's Report, a leading morning journal, with characteristic enterprise, dispatched one of its most reliable correspondents to make a tour of the Erie road and investigate its condition thoroughly, with a view to test the accuracy of the statements put forward by the President. After a thorough examination of the entire line, the correspondent, who had started with a most unfavorable impression, and the full conviction that he would be able to pick Mr. Gould's report to pieces, found himself in a rather embarrassing predicament. So much had been written and said against the road, its condition had been so shamefully misrepresented, and the erroneous impressions prevailed so extensively that he foresaw that the man who first dared to publish an impartial statement would have considerable difficulty in proving himself a disinterested observer. To his credit be it said, the correspondent decided to proclaim the truth at all risks. Being an old *attache*, and a man of unimpeachable integrity, he escaped the suspicion which would certainly have attached to one less tried and trusty, but nevertheless, the fact that his close scrutiny developed nothing in corroboration of the unfavorable statements advanced by the opponents of Gould and Fisk, but on the contrary, revealed so much in favor of the present Erie management, occasioned such intense surprise in all quarters, and particularly in the editorial sanctum of the journal referred to, that the impartial commissioner was hurriedly recalled. On making the explanation required of him, the correspondent submitted conclusive evidence that he had not been imposed upon, or biased in any way, and was deservedly commended for his courageous attempt to shame the patron saint of the speculators and monopolists who have leagued themselves against the men who saved Erie from bankruptcy and raised it to its present proud position as the first railroad of the American continent. The stockholders and bondholders of the Erie Railway are even more indebted to this fearless correspondent than President Gould or Comptroller Fisk himself.

Until recently, the President of Erie and his able coadjutors have paid little or no heed to the slanders promulgated by their Wall Street enemies and parties interested in rival lines; while for the blind and blundering censure of ignorant outsiders they manifested the utmost unconcern. It was only when their unscrupulous adversaries adopted the expedient of subsidizing the more corrupt portion of the public press, and, exasperated at finding that mere personal attacks failed to further their ulterior designs, commenced promulgating false and malicious charges, *calculated to injure the credit of the corporation*, that Gould and Fisk awoke to the necessity of taking some notice of these dastardly attacks. As regards themselves individually, confident that success would gild their efforts, however extraordinary, these much-enduring men remained indifferent—too indifferent, as they at last realized, to personal attacks, while devoting themselves, with all the marvelous energy for which they are alike famous, to the two grand ends they had in view—the reconstruction of the Erie road and the restoration of the ruined credit of the corporation. Let their bitterest enemies, the managers of rival railways, answer as to whether or no they have succeeded in accomplishing the first of these Herculean tasks, and let the stockholders, American and foreign, who have been so egregiously imposed upon by the enemies of Erie, make thorough and impartial investigation of the financial policy of the present administration before delegating the second task to less able, and, may be, far less reliable hands.

Since the "Erie Princes" became famous, it may be said they have been on trial at the bar of public opinion. Their every word has been noted and every movement chronicled, for they have been subject to the strictest surveillance of the press. They have been portrayed by Jenkins and pestered by interviewers—written up and written down, over and over again; and now that we have such an abundance of evidence concerning them, it is about time to close the case for the prosecution.

There is no need for elaborate argument in behalf of the accused; they rely confidently upon the stubbornness of the facts which are to speak for them, and believe that in the plainest statement of a fact there is a superlative eloquence which effectually disposes of the weak inventions of their enemies.

THE REAL ENEMIES OF ERIE.

The English shareholders, in their utter ignorance of the history of the Erie Corporation, make the absurd mistake of blaming the present managers for the crimes of their predecessors. It must be remembered that Messrs. Gould and Fisk have been but a very short time in office, and it must be admitted, even by the most jaundiced of their opponents, that during their brief term they have worked a vast amount more good than evil to the property entrusted to their care. This latter fact is patent to all who have given the affairs of the road sufficient attention to enable them to form an opinion, and, consequently, no one will be more benefitted by the discoveries of a *really* thorough and impartial investigation, than the men who are accused of throwing every obstacle in the way of such a proceeding. Of those who are interested in the welfare of Erie, none are so anxious to have the condition of the magnificent property of the corporation thoroughly ventilated as the more responsible members of the present management. Much and wrongfully as these officers have been abused, the speedy and vigorous prosecution of the proposed investigation is a consummation devoutly to be wished, and the publication of the result a matter of simple justice. But when so many powerful cliques are struggling against the best interests of the Corporation for their own base purposes, the difficulty is in finding men who will make full and fair examination, and honest report. To none others will the present managers afford the necessary facilities.

Absurd as is the mistake made by the English party it is in a measure excusable, seeing how grossly they have been imposed upon by the agents of the two men, of all others, Drew and Vanderbilt, whose insatiable greed has been to Erie the "direful spring of woes unnumbered." The disastrous results of the operations of this wonderfully well-matched pair of veteran financiers are too well known on this side to be recapitulated here; but it is about time our cousins over the water posted themselves a little on this head. Let them but take the pains to ascertain the condition of the road under preceding administrations, and they will have the whole thing at a glance, and be able to realize the fact that Drew brought the corporation to the verge of bankruptcy, and that the present management saved the road from ruin and Vanderbilt. Those who desire to be impartial, must have the previous history of this great national artery of commerce in view, while passing judgment upon the present administration. Thanks to the persistent misrepresentations of their opponents,

Gould and Fisk were condemned before they were even called upon to give an account of their stewardship.

Until recently, it has been the fashion to abuse the present managers of Erie whenever occasion could be made, but fortunately the thing was carried too far—their opponents overdid it, and the public tired of it. Then, and not till then, (" better late than never," however,) the question arose, " What have they done to deserve it ?" That question has been *replied to* in many ways; but as far as the interests of the Erie Corporation are concerned, the defamers of Messrs. Gould and Fisk have yet to *answer* it. There is abundant proof that those who took the initiative in trumping up accusations against the so-called Erie Princes, were actuated by a desire to further their own ends rather than the interests of the Corporation, notwithstanding their loud-protested devotion to the latter; but it is equally evident that a large proportion of those who joined in the recent senseless outcry, did so "for the mere fun of the thing," much as people sometimes join in the cry of " mad dog," when, for all they know to the contrary, the unfortunate object of their clamors may be more self-possessed than his pursuers. Fortunately for the road, the men who have undertaken to restore its fallen fortunes are remarkable for coolness and indomitable will, and, adhering to the masterly plan they had originally mapped out, they pursued the tenor of their way, swerving neither to the right nor left, until they had saved Erie from all danger of absorption by rival corporations, and secured such connections as make their line the highway of the Continent. It is possible that at some time or other the enemies of Erie may triumph, and deprive the present incumbents of office, but they cannot deprive them of the credit of having battled bravely for the road in the most critical period of its eventful history, established its independence on an enduring basis, and made it at once the greatest and best line in the country. If, on the other hand, the control of this great national thoroughfare is left to the men who have in the marvelously short space of twelve months raised it from ruin to its present prosperous condition, until they have had time to fully develop its resources, and realize their dreams of its glorious future, neither Fisk nor Gould will be under the necessity of putting up their own monuments. They will deserve a bronze memorial apiece—one at New York and the other at San Francisco, where the western terminus of Erie is destined to be located at no distant date.

Indeed, the stockholders of Erie, American and foreign, may congratulate themselves upon the fact that their property is in the hands of men of rare ability—men who seem to have been specially endowed for the great and responsible work which has fallen upon them. Fisk and Gould being so thoroughly posted in the intricacies of American finance, and the ways of Wall Street, no better men could be found to defend the interests of the corporation from the rapacity of the speculative cliques who have done so much to damage its credit, both at home and abroad. Then, in addition to their other qualifications, they have proved themselves to be the most able and progressive railroad men of the day. Certainly no line in the United States was more in need of good management than the Erie was when they assumed control, while to-day it is in every respect a model for all others.

Now that the public is so thoroughly posted as to the affairs of the road, and so intimately acquainted with its able managers the designs of the disappointed ones who have been at the bottom of all the recent troubles and misrepresentation are revealed in all their enormity.

Drew, in his seventeen years more or less criminal mismanagement, had things all his own way. Few persons interested themselves in the affairs of the corporation then but the stockholders, and they were easily pacified with paltry dividends and deluded with cheap promises whenever they ventured to be at all inquisitive or complaining. In what Mr. Drew calls "the good old times," the press was not quite as vigilant as it is now, and consequently the general public were in blissful ignorance of the unsatisfactory condition of the finances of the Erie Company. The ruinous state of the line and its rolling stock of course did not escape notice, but the management was criminally indifferent on this head and so there was no help for it. To-day it is different. Such a broad flood of light is directed on the affairs of Erie by the press and the courts, that no move, however slight, on the part of its management, escapes attention and criticism, and consequently Gould and Fisk could not follow the examples set by those of their predecessors who *did* plunder the corporation, were they so minded. The legal war of 1868 made Erie famous, and the brilliant triumph which Gould and Fisk gained over their unscrupulous opponents, Drew and Vanderbilt, gave them a world-wide reputation. Drew was fairly beaten off, and Vanderbilt, to his shame be it said, consented to be paid off. To those who take exception to the manner in which the ancient mariner of Staten Island and the ex-drover of Putnam County were made to relinquish their clutches on the Erie treasury it may be remarked that violent diseases need violent treatment. True the remedy in such extreme cases is sometimes more disastrous than the evil, but the prosperous condition of Erie at the present time proves that its case was in good hands.

EXIT RAMSEY & CO.

Subsequent to the publication of the second Chapter of Erie the Ramseyites have suffered a complete rout. The secret history of the action brought by Mr. Ramsey against "the leading conspirators *in* the present Erie management" has already been made public, and the revelations made during the trial plainly demonstrated that the leading conspirators *against* the present management are the real enemies of the Erie stockholders. The Ramsey party failed ignominiously, as they deserved—their charges being so utterly absurd as to make all connected with them ridiculous, and their pretence of championing the rights of the "stockholders and bondholders generally" being too transparent to deceive anybody. The result of this abortive attempt to place Mr. Groesbeck in control of the Erie treasury proved how accurate was Mr. Fisk's summary of the case as given in the previous chapter. In saying that it could not be characterized as malicious because it was so utterly ridiculous the genial Prince of Erie and jovial Admiral of the Narragansett navy was a trifle too charitable. But then Mr. Fisk is ever prone to err on the side of charity. The fact is, Messrs. Ramsey & Co. expended a great deal of malice in the prosecution of this suit, but fortunately it proved impotent. The confessions, extorted from the principal conspirators on examination under oath, give a sufficient insight into their plot to prove who were sinning and who sinned against.

The following charges, made by the Ramsey faction—the only clique, by the way, which had the hardihood to attack Gould and Fisk on their strongest point, the management of the road—are specimen splashes of the mud so continuously showered at the "powers that be" by the more envious and spiteful of the powers that were, and the more mendacious of the powers that would be.

1. The said persons and their confederates have made no material additions to the earnings of the road.

2. Little or nothing has been done in the way of extending the line, or improving its equipment.

3. Their management has not been attended with any gain of cheapness, safety or comfort in transportation.

4. The employes of the road have become demoralized, and less serviceable, and its net earnings have diminished.

5. The present managers are extremely unpopular among the employes of the road.

6. There are an unusual and needless number of ill-advised and unjust business arrangements, relative to the affairs of the said Company, and its relations with competing roads are needlessly unfriendly and disadvantageous.

Each of the above deliberate falsehoods, and others too numerous to recapitulate, are effectually disposed of by the irresistible array of impressive facts and unanswerable figures, set forth in President Gould's remarkably clear and business-like Report. But, notwithstanding the absence of any supporting evidence, they had currency, and found believers for a time, and similar slanders, equally groundless, prevail to-day. However, to use one of Mr. Fisk's favorite quotations, "The truth is mighty and must prevail."

Now, then, it may be asked, whose fault is it that the Erie management became somewhat unpopular for a time, and that there was a consequent "loss of patronage, confidence and earnings"? Whose fault but the men who were guilty of manufacturing and circulating the atrocious slanders which have done so much damage to the credit of the Erie corporation both at home and abroad?

And another question. Had Fisk and Gould been as black as they were painted in the subsidised journals referred to, would it not have been better policy for the parties interested in the welfare of the road to have held their peace until they had secured a sufficient majority to remove them? But no, the "irreconcilables" who have waged such merciless war against the present dynasty, recked little how much ruin they worked, provided they could only fasten their greedy clutches on the earnings of the road. And now that speculators on this side have been foiled at every turn and forced to seek "fresh fields and pastures new," the foreign stockholders are urged by a contemptible ring of English speculators to pursue the same suicidal course. But since Gould and Fisk have so bravely battled it out with the different American cliques and conquered all domestic difficulties, it would be something like a national disgrace if Erie were allowed to fall under British rule. There is no fear of this, however,—the Oneida on which the irrepressible Admiral has determined to sink or swim is not destined to be destroyed by the piratical Bombay commanded by Barrister Burt—for already the foreigners begin to realize the mortifying fact that they have been grossly deceived, and have discovered that, all things considered, Fisk and Gould are the right men in the right place.

ERIE UNDER THE OLD REGIME.

THE TRACK IN 1868.

Reference has been made to the ruinous condition into which the road had been allowed to fall under the criminal mismanagement of the previous administration. Evidence on this head is embarrassingly abundant, but the following official documents alone will be sufficient to prove that the sins of the old regime have been visited on the new.

OFFICE GENERAL SUPERINTENDENT,
NEW YORK, March 3, 1868.

HON. JOHN S. ELDRIDGE,
President Erie Railway:

SIR:—On the 3d of December, I addressed a communication to the Vice-President, recommending the purchase of 5,000 tons of steel rails, and at an interview with you, I expressed the opinion that 15,000 to 18,000 tons of rails would be required for the repairs of track during the year 1868.

Since that opinion was given, we have passed through three months of unusually severe winter weather, and moved more than an average winter tonnage, with the road-bed frozen solid as a rock, the rails encased in snow and ice, so that it has been impossible to do much in the way of repairs; the iron rails have broken, laminated and worn out beyond all precedent, until *there is scarce a mile of your road, except that laid with steel rails, between Jersey City and Salamanca or Buffalo, where it is safe to run a train at the ordinary passenger-train speed,* and many portions of the road can only be traversed safely by reducing the speed of all trains to 12 or 15 miles per hour, solely on account of the worn out and rotten condition of the rails. Broken wheels, axles, engines and trains off the track, have been of daily, *almost hourly*, occurrence for the last two months, caused mostly by defective rails. Fully one thousand *broken rails* were taken from the track in the month of January, while the number removed on account of lamination, crushing or wearing out was much greater. February will show a still worse record than January.

The failure of rails is confined to no particular make, although there is a difference, easily observed, between those made at Scranton and those re-rolled at Elmira. The former break readily into many pieces, and by so doing are pretty sure to throw a train from the track; a large number of these rails have broken with less than six months' service, some with scarce one month's wear.

With the track laid with the John Brown Bessemer Steel, no fault need be found. But one rail has broken during the winter, and no lamination, and very little wear is perceptible. Twenty steel rails were laid in Jersey City yard last March, the iron rails adjoining, subject to the same wear, have been renewed four times since the steel was put down, and I have no doubt the steel rails will outlast three times as many more iron rails.

This winter's experience has satisfied me that the quality and weight of the iron rails in use cannot be depended upon to sustain the traffic of the Erie Railway. Forty-two ton locomotives hauling trains of fifty and sixty loaded cars, and passenger engines weighing thirty-seven tons, running at a speed of thirty to forty miles per hour, literally crush and grind out the iron rails beneath them. Instances have been reported to me of rails removed from track too much worn for safety, where the first imperfection was visible but the day before.

In view of this state of things, what is the remedy? Manifestly the adoption of steel rails as far as practicable, and iron rails of superior quality and heavier section, to be followed by the gradual reduction of the weight of engines and cars as new equipment becomes necessary. The tendency of late years has been to larger and more powerful locomotives, and heavier, stronger cars, and this has been carried to such an extent as to render them out of all proportion to the strength and durability of track. Especially has this been the fact upon the Erie Railway.

The condition of the iron at the present date *is such as to give me much anxiety and apprehension for the safety of trains. We cannot and do not attempt to make the schedule time with our trains, nearly all lose from two to five hours in passing over the road, and it has been only by the exercise of extreme caution we have been able thus far to escape serious accident.*

A very large quantity of rails must be laid as soon as the weather will permit and they can be furnished.

In conclusion I desire to modify my estimate of the quantity of rails required for the current year. After a careful observation of the whole road, assisted by information obtained from Division Superintendents and Track Masters, I have come to the conclusion that twenty-five thousand tons of rails will be needed to keep up your track in 1868, and I would earnestly recommend that as large a proportion as possible shall be of steel.

Very respectfully your obedient servant,

H. RIDDLE,

General Sup't.

INADEQUATE MOTIVE POWER.

OFFICE GENERAL SUPERINTENDENT,

NEW YORK, March 3, 1868.

HON. J. S. ELDRIDGE,

President Erie Railway Co.,

SIR:—A careful review of the present condition of the Motive Power of the Erie Railway Company enables me to present the following statement for your consideration:

The company own 371 locomotives—of this number about 30 are condemned as entirely useless, and some 40 more are of but little value, owing to their long service and general infirmity, being considered unsafe to carry even moderate steam pressure, and sure to break down if run long distances. 220 engines have performed over ten years service, and 143 of that number over 15 years service. The master mechanics report 128 of these locomotives as requiring new boilers, and recommend the complete reconstruction of 107 of the number whenever the boilers shall be renewed, or in other words, instead of giving the old engine a new boiler, it is deemed more to the interest of the company to construct a complete new engine, for the following reasons: most of these engines are of the kind known as half-crank engines, an expensive and troublesome class to keep in repair. The engines having been so long in service *no dependence can be placed upon the strength and durability of any of their parts*—they are of a great variety of patterns, and make it necessary to keep a very large stock of material on hand to provide against breakages, there being something over sixty different kinds of engines on the Erie road.

It will be seen by the foregoing, that the Company have only 300 serviceable engines, considerably less than that of really efficient ones. From 15 to 25 per cent. are in shops undergoing repairs, ordinarily, at this season often a larger proportion. Our mechanics estimate the life of an engine at 15 years. Assuming that to be true, we should build 20 every year to keep our 300 good, to say nothing of the 70 now idle and worthless; but as we have added by purchase and construction only 12 new engines to our stock, during the last two years, we are at the present moment *some* 28 *engines short* of what we should have to make good the depreciation. In view therefore of the certain increase of the coal tonnage, and probable increase of both through and way traffic, I feel justified in saying there should be 50 new locomotives added to the equipment of the road during the next twelve months. In the Company's shops at Susquehanna and Dunkirk, if worked to their capacity, with a slight increase of machinery, it is estimated 30 engines per annum can be built—at present we are working only force sufficient to build about one-third that number. The engines built in the Company's shops, in point of strength, durability and perfection of workmanship, far excel those procured from locomotive builders, and while their cost may fully equal, perhaps exceed, the price for which similar engines may be constructed for, I yet deem it good policy to fully employ our own facilities for the construction of engines.

To fill out the number I have ventured to suggest as needed, 20 will be required outside of the Company's ability to construct. These I would contract for to be built after specifications and plans to be furnished by the Company's officers, and under the inspection of a good mechanic to be selected and paid by the Railway Company. In this way I think we could obtain satisfactory machines.

I also deem it my duty to recommend an increase of Freight and Coal cars: say 300 Box Freight cars and 100 Coal cars, in adaddition to those heretofore ordered.

The Coal cars are sure to be needed, and the Box Freight cars, unless the freight traffic should fall off contrary to all expectations.

Respectfully your obedient servant,

H. RIDDLE, *General Sup't.*

P. S.—Since writing the foregoing Report, I have learned from General Potter that he is desirous of establishing stock yards at Urbana and Cincinnati, on the line of the Atlantic and Great Western Railway, and taking stock for the New York market that has hitherto gone via Pittsburgh, provided the Erie will furnish her full proportion of stock cars. This we cannot do without adding, say 200 stock cars to our present number, and to meet this and other demands I would respectfully submit the following estimate for new cars:

300 Box Cars, - - -	at $800	$240,000
200 Box Cattle Cars, - -	" 900	180,000
100 Coal Dumps, - - -	" 625	62,500
		$482,500

Rival corporations profited immensely at the expense of Erie, by publishing the above damaging reports of the dangerous condition of its track, and the utter inadequacy of its motive power as advertisements of the superiority of their respective lines. In fact its passenger traffic has not yet recovered, although to-day the accommodations of the Erie line far surpass those of any other railway in the world. Thanks to the careful nursing of Gould and Fisk, however, this branch of the business is now steadily increasing, and the earnings will soon be a long way ahead of previous figures. The freight business, increased by recent extensions and connections, is already in excess of the most sanguine expectations of Gould himself, and consequently far beyond the wildest dreams of the fossils of the old regime.

After reading the foregoing documents and President Gould's Report, the most prejudiced must be convinced that the road is now under able and efficient management, and that untiring efforts have been made and are still being made, to advance the credit of the corporation. No wonder that the road lost patronage, and that its reputation was of the worst—the wonder is that so much has been done to increase its business and improve its condition in so short a time. Whatever may be the faults of Fisk and Gould, and, bold as the assertion may be in view of the countless accusations which have been put forward, nothing of a serious nature has yet been *proved* against them—the Erie stockholders will do well to retain them in office until they are *perfectly certain* of obtaining better men to succeed them. This is a point which cannot be too carefully considered.

THE SECOND CHAPTER OF ERIE.

"Trade now dominates the world, and railways dominate trade," says the author of the first "Chapter of Erie," and, accepting this hypothesis as correct, it follows that the men who dominate railways, dominate pretty nearly all that is worth dominating in this mundane sphere. There are countries where railway presidents and directors are held subject to the laws of governments, which are jealous governments, and will not tolerate the worship of any other powers but their own; but here, owing to certain little defects in "the best government the world ever saw," railway rule is becoming stronger every day, and, in default of check, will soon be paramount. If current reports are to be believed, the State of New York affords the most remarkable instance of the kind of *imperium in imperio* referred to, yet developed. The "Erie ring," then, being such a "power in the land" for good or evil, and the Erie road being one of the great lines of travel and commerce, the public cannot know too much concerning the men who rule Erie, and the manner in which they wield the tremendous power vested in them and discharge their respective duties.

James Fisk, Jr., and Jay Gould have figured so frequently in the public prints during the past two years that their names have become as "familiar as household words," but as they were first forced into notoriety in connection with their veteran opponents, Cornelius Vanderbilt and Daniel Drew, in consequence of the extraordinary legal, and other proceedings, which marked the exciting contest for the control of the Erie road, and latterly in connection with Abel R. Corbin, General Butterfield and others, concerned in the recent gigantic gold-ring conspiracy, the fact that Messrs. Fisk and Gould have the business and working of the Erie Railway under their immediate control has been generally overlooked. They have been discussed and criticised as financiars and speculators; some censuring their conduct, some applauding them, but all astounded at the grandeur of their schemes. Fisk has been "written up" repeatedly in his character of speculator, operatic manager, and admiral, but of his rendition of his principal role—that of a "railway manager"—little or no notice has been taken. So far as his connection with the business af the Erie road goes, Mr. Gould has also escaped attention hitherto. The object of this Second Chapter of Erie is to show how the road is worked under the present dynasty, and how far Messrs. Gould and Fisk are qualified for the responsible positions to which they have been elected. With this highly important end in view, the writer has recently made a close and careful survey of the entire line, not omitting even the smallest of its numerous branches, and the information thus obtained will enable the reader to draw his own conclusions as to whether or no the Erie princes fail in their duties as servants of the travelling public.

ERIE HISTORY.

The history of the Erie Railway has been, indeed, a checkered one, and if written in full, would be as instructing as interesting. But great as its financial difficulties have been, or may yet be, they can never be at all commensurate with the physical difficulties which were surmounted or removed by the indomitable energy of its constructors. Scaling lofty mountains, skirting rugged precipices, skimming through fertile valleys, and bridging broad rivers—connecting the Hudson, the Susquehanna, the St. Lawrence and the Ohio, and spreading its terminal branches along the shores of Lakes Erie and Ontario, well has it been said that this magnificent monument of national enterprise is as important in our civilization as was the Appian Way in the "most high and palmy days of Rome."

The financial troubles of Erie commenced long before Messrs. Gould and Fisk became connected with the line, and *apropos* of this fact, it may be parenthetically remarked that financial troubles are as inevitable in the early days of railway corporations as measles in infancy. The difficulties which resulted in the titanic conflict of 1868 had their origin as far back as 1850, when Mr. Daniel Drew first took his seat in the directory and commenced manipulating the stock, and culminated in consequence of Vanderbilt's manœuvres to obtain absolute control of the Erie road in order to establish a gigantic monopoly by which he could lock the vast trade of the West in his iron arms. At any rate, all accounts agree that when "the cruel war" was over, and in accordance with terms upon which the settlement was effected, Messrs. Fisk and Gould assumed the control of the Erie Railway, they found its treasury empty, and its reputation ragged in the extreme. "It may well be believed," says the author of the First Chapter of Erie, "that Messrs. Fisk and Gould could not have regarded their empty treasury, just depleted to the extent of nine millions—trust funds misapplied by directors in the process of stock gambling—without serious question as to their ability to save the road from bankruptcy." But the road *was* saved from bankruptcy; and to-day there is abundant evidence to show that it is in a fair way of becoming, ere long, the most prosperous line in the country. Gould and Fisk boldly undertook the apparently hopeless task of engineering the Erie corporation through the financial difficulties which impeded the working of its existing lines, and blocked its destined path through the fertile valleys and growing cities of the far West, and the sequel so far as it has been developed, has demonstrated that they are men fully as skillful, energetic, and persevering in their respective ways as were the engineers who blasted their path over the rugged heights of the Shawangunk ridge, scaled the perpendicular precipices along the Delaware, and ran their line to stations 1,800 feet above the level of the sea, and thence to the objective points on the lake shores.

THE INDEPENDENCE OF ERIE.

Nor Drew nor Vanderbilt believed in the possibility of maintaining the independence of Erie after the crisis of 1868, but up to the present Messrs. Gould and Fisk have held their own against all comers, and even their bitterest opponents cannot but admire the extraordinary abilities they have displayed. Deplorable, however, as was the depletion of the treasury at the time that Vanderbilt and Drew concluded to compromise with their opponents and abandon the struggle they had so remorselessly waged for the control of Erie, the dangerous condition and defective equipment of the road was a subject for still wider and deeper lamentation. Only stockholders and speculators were affected by the grievous reduction of the company's finances, but the ruinous condition into which the road and all connected therewith had been allowed to fall, was a public calamity. Mr. Fisk, who, like his predecessor, Drew, and his wily antagonist, Vanderbilt, is evidently a believer in the Jesuit dogma, that "the end justifies the means," makes no secret of the *modus operandi* by which the treasury was refilled, and the much-neglected machinery of the Erie road lubricated and put in running order; so that it now works, as all who make examination must admit, far smoother, and more profitably than at any previous period in its history. Whatever complaints the Erie stockholders may have against Messrs. Fisk and Gould, on account of stock manipulations, &c., are matters in which the traveling public and the traders and manufacturers who freight the trains on this great national thoroughfare have very little concern. The morality of Wall Street is a distinct virtue, peculiar to the locality, and professed only by those who are engaged in the more or less questionable transactions to which it alone applies. The outside public cannot consistently be called upon to render decisions in cases where breaches of this unique virtue are alleged, and consequently all matter pertaining to the charges of "watering stock," "gold-cornering operations," "unlawful appropriation of funds," &c., &c., which have been preferred against Messrs. Fisk and Gould and their associates in the Erie directory, must be ruled out of this chapter as altogether irrelevant.

In the cases referred to, were they guilty of all the "irregularities" of which they stand accused, it would be hard to decide—blamelessness giving priority, by virtue of the scriptural precedent, which of their many accusers would be entitled to the privilege of casting the first stone at them. In the case in hand, however, Jay Gould and James Fisk, Jr., are arraigned before the public solely in their capacities as "railway men"—as the parties directly responsible for the conduct of the vast business of the Erie road.

First and foremost among the accusers stands one Joseph H. Ramsey, who had a "little difficulty" with Messrs. Fisk and Gould, respecting the directorship of the Albany and Susquehanna Railroad. Mr. Ramsey having purposely purchased a small quantity of Erie stock, and been furnished with a bond or two, was induced by certain parties who are desirous of ousting some of the present incumbents, and securing for themselves positions as directors, to commence an action "on behalf of the stockholders and bondholders" generally, against Jay Gould, James Fisk, Jr., Frederick A. Lane, "and other leading conspirators in the present management." From the carefully prepared abstract of the multitudinous charges crammed into the complaint entered in this case, the following are selected as the only points on which the people who are in the habit of traveling over, or of doing business with the Erie Railway are at all seriously interested.

THE ACCUSATIONS.

Concerning the defendants as "railway men," Mr. Ramsey alleges, that while "the said three persons and their confederates" have largely increased the common stock of the Erie Railway Company, no material additions have been made to the earnings of the road, and little or nothing has been done in the way of extending the line or improving its equipment; that their management of the road has not been attended with any advance of its credit or good name, "or with any advantage to any class of creditors, or with any gain of cheapness, safety, or comfort in transportation on its road; but, on the contrary, and as the result of the abuses of the defendants, transportation on said road has been visited with calamities of unusual horror, damage and death; the credit of said Company has been impaired, and its good repute has been injured; its most experienced and valuable servants have been forced from self-respect to seek employment elsewhere; its creditors have suffered loss, delay and vexation; its employes are becoming demoralized and less serviceable; its stock and bonds have greatly fallen in all the markets of the world, and its net earnings have diminished, while all its rival roads have made increase in such earnings, and have had their stock greatly advanced in all such markets, and the Erie Railway, and its managers in such period, have become in the highest degree unpopular and disreputable, to the great loss of patronage, confidence, credit and earnings. That several of the most efficient and experienced men, long in prominent positions in the employment of said Company, have, in self-respect, been compelled to resign their places, rather than hold them subject to such demands as said three persons made upon them; and by reason thereof, the discipline of the men on the line is much impaired; that there are an unusual and needless number of ill-advised and unjust business arrangements relative to the affairs of said Company; the men on the line are dissatisfied; their most experienced, able and superior executive officers have been driven away, and strikes and other combinations are constant, increasing, and of threatening proportions, and the relations of the Company with competing roads are needlessly unfreindly and disadvantageous to the Erie Railway Company. That said three persons are extremely unpopular among the employes of the Company, and are by them, when they think it safe to do so, severely blamed; and the agents of the road generally regard said three persons as having impaired the public respect for the said Corporation and its road, and as having disgraced the corporate name; and for such reasons all said persons are under less discipline, serving the Company less efficiently, and many of them have all the more readily engaged in the recent strikes and dangerous combinations lately so much more frequent than formerly existing along the road; and the great body of the disinterested bond and stockholders and creditors of said Company, and the better public sentiment of the people of New York, hold said three persons in abhorence, and consider it a public disgrace and wrong that they are allowed to control said corporation."

The real origin and principal object of the Ramsey suit are revealed by the fact, that the documents setting forth the above charges, were prepared in the office of the private attorney of the President of the New York Central.

THE BALLET-GIRL CHARGES.

Now, although there is a superabundance of matter in the complaint, about scantily attired ballet-girls dancing around the desks of the railway office to the lascivious strains of lutes, dulcimers, and all kinds of wind and string instruments, while the demoralized clerks and attaches are accused of singing time-tables set to opera bouffe melodies, and otherwise disporting themselves with an outrageous disregard to the proprieties of business—and a sufficient amount of similar nonsense to warrant the belief that the whole thing is simply a burlesque, written to order, for the purpose of affording a vehicle for the promulgation of the false and malicious statements concerning the working of the Erie road, which have been concocted in the interest of rival lines and parties—yet public interest requires that the actual condition of the road—good, bad, or indifferent—should at once be investigated and published for the benefit of those who intrust life and property to the care of those responsible for its working. The comparatively unimportant questions between the Erie managers and their disaffected stockholders are matters for the courts to decide at some time or other, but the charges concerning the road are matters which require immediate investigation and thorough ventilation. However, before submitting the evidence collected on this point, let us hear what the accused have to say for themselves, accepting Mr. Fisk as their spokesman.

A VOICE FROM ERIE.

"We have never done anything—we have never attempted to do anything—but there was somebody to find fault with it for the mere reason, as it seemed, that we had done or attempted to do it." With this preliminary protest, the irrepressible Admiral proceeds as follows: "The first thing we found in our investigation of Erie matters was a very well 'dusted' treasury. We were next made aware that on each side of Erie there existed antagonistic lines, which were aiming at its speedy absorption. We resolved to preserve the independence of the road, and to do all that lay in our power to extend it. But we found that our equipment was altogether inadequate to our work. We needed more engines, more cars, and the track was in bad order. The trouble was there was not money to carry up and complete the foundations that had been laid. As we went on our need for money became more pressing. I did not stop to run and ask my mother how I should get it—the first thing was to get it—get it. I knew if we got it at all, we should get it right. Well, we issued convertible bonds, the proceeds of which enabled us to put the road in good order and extend the lines, connections and business. We kept on selling bonds, and have paid out, on the Erie Railway bills that have been audited, fourteen millions of dollars. These fourteen millions have been expended on the road, its equipments, its engines, its cars, its steel rails, its road-beds, its connections, and in increasing its business conveniences. This has been done notwithstanding the great plannings and plottings, mandamuses and injunctions of our opponents. Mr. Gould has in all this been entitled to a great deal more credit than I. His head is long enough to control and carry out all the projects he undertakes; but it may be well enough, you know, to have a little assistance, and I have assisted him a little. We didn't suppose that money could be created and paid out in such magnitude without making a world of comments, but we paid little heed to comments. We were pushing on our railroad, making our connections and getting ready to do our work. We have a good road to-day, and can do an enormous amount of work with it. The road earned for the year ending September 30, 1869, $18,790,905, against $14,376,-872 for the year ending September 30, 1868. How's that? An increase of three and a quarter million dollars! No wonder Messrs. Vanderbilt, Ramsey & Co. swear we are neglecting the interests of the road, and 'damaging and demoralizing everything in general.' It seems to me that if we continue 'fighting it out on that line,' we shall succeed in 'damaging and demoralizing' the monopolists who are now in league against us. We'll try, anyhow,"

THE ERIE RAILWAY SHALL GO ON.

"We don't care how low the competing lines on each side of us put down their rates, we can run our road to-day and haul our freight cheaper than they can, if they *are* forty years older. We shall go on with the Erie Railway as we have been going. If there are others that own, or have larger interests in it, let them come and take charge and we will stand aside. As long as we have the control we will do our best to break up the monopoly that charges one dollar and eighty cents per hundred for freight, and three dollars on a barrel of flour from Chicago to New York. We are content to abide by the voice of the majority of the stock; but don't see any reason, if we can manage the Erie road why we should give it up. We are doing all we can for it. If our ideas are wrong, sooner or later the road will pass into other hands. At any rate we are doing no harm in laying steel rails, building comfortable cars, and in making travel safe and pleasant. The accidents which have occurred are not attributable to want of care on the part of the company, but to the villany of the man Bowen in the Carr's Rock disaster, and to the negligence of an engineer at Mast Hope. The Erie is the greatest corporation on the American continent, and is as vital to the welfare of New York City as the Croton water is to her comfort and safety.

" As to this Ramsey case it amounts to nothing. He has been at law with us for several months respecting the possession and directorship of the Albany and Susquehanna Railroad. Being unfriendly towards us, and having more or less influence with certain county judges, he was imported from Albany by some of our Wall Street enemies, and furnished with a little stock in order to enable him to harrass us, and produce a counter-irritation to this suit now pending at Rochester. D. B. Eaton, who is engaged as Ramsey's attorney, was dismissed by us from the Erie service for causes for which the company is now sueing him. The 100 page complaint, of which they furnished their own abstracts to all the city papers, contains hardly anything calling for a serious reply—the greater portion of it being a mass of absurdities—one cannot call it malicious, it being so completely ridiculous. In order to put us to greater trouble and inconvenience, Ramsey was sent off to Delhi, in the County of Delaware, the most out-of-the-way place in the State, being 40 miles from the Erie road, 20 miles from the Albany and Susquehanna, and 150 miles from the residence of any person who could be a witness in the case. By swearing 'upon information and belief,' Ramsey procured from his friend Judge Murray, one of the most extraordinary injunctions ever heard of. Judge Murray was then a member of the Court of Appeals, and was not obliged to act at all in the Supreme Court. Generally speaking I find the press to be tolerably fair and impartial, but in this case I think the papers which have abused the judge who thought it his duty to grant an order giving us a moment's time to answer a complaint of 100 pages or so, which has taken malicious parties and learned attorneys months to concoct and draft, have not taken a proper view of the matter."

CONDITION OF THE ROAD.

The people who are most competent to give information as to the actual condition of the Erie road are those who are engaged in working it, and those who are most in the habit of travelling over it. The former class will, of course, make their testimony as favorable as possible to their employers, and the latter will be more likely to exaggerate in blaming than in praising. While engaged in making a thorough survey of the lines and works, the writer availed himself of every opportunity of conversing with the company's servants, and of comparing notes with fellow passengers. The men engaged on the line make only one serious complaint against the management, and that is the excessive severity of the discipline now enforced, and the rigor of the rules which Messrs. Fisk and Gould, and their Division Superintendents, have framed to insure " eternal vigilance " and the faithful discharge of the respective duties of their subordinates. The patrons of the road make no other complaint than that one or two serious accidents have occurred. Those most conversant with the affairs of the road admit, however, that it would be wrong to lay the blame of those disasters upon Messrs. Fisk and Gould, knowing, as they do, how much the road has been improved by the present managers, and what great exertions are being made to improve it still further.

THE FUTURE OF THE ERIE RAILWAY.

It needs only a glance at the map to convince one that the Erie Railway is destined to be the grand highway for the Western portion of this continent. The glorious future of the interminable and all-embracing network of rail, of which the Erie of to-day, great and important as it is already acknowledged to be, is but the parent stem, is an interesting and pleasing subject for the contemplation of such as take a patriotic concern in the welfare of this country, and desire to see the present altogether inadequate facilities for communication between the different sections of the republic speedily improved upon, and our railway system brought as near perfection as possible. It needs no prophet to tell us that the Erie Railway will soon be to the continent what Broadway is to New York —a central artery whose tributary branches ramify the most out-of-the-way corners and vitalize the most remote extremities. Eminent foreign engineers and competent native authorities concur in the opinion that the Erie is one of the best constructed roads in America, and when it is considered that its broad gauge double-track already unites the great Lakes with New York—the destined commercial centre of the world—and connects all the important lines of the productive West with the great Eastern centres of trade and manufactures, who can doubt the glorious future of Erie? What can obstruct its manifest destiny as the great business thoroughfare of the iron age? Nothing. It is already the principal thoroughfare for the teeming products of the mighty West in their transit to the sea. It is much to be marvelled at that the men who helped to bring into existence this vast artery of trade and travel, and those who have hitherto had control of it, should have contented themselves with uniting New York with Lake Erie, and never have made any effort to push forward and grasp the colossal fortunes awaiting them in the West. Evidently they were not up to the age in which we live. The present managers, are men of the period, however—a little in advance if anything. With a deep and well-founded faith in the glorious commercial future of the country, these men have bent themselves to the task of securing a continuous line of railroad penetrating the very heart of the immense agricultural basin of the Ohio River, and thence, following the course of the empire of civilization to the shores of the Pacific. In getting the control of the Atlantic and Great Western, they have made their first successful step towards securing the business of the rich regions lying east and west of the Mississippi River. Despite the genius and energy of the late management, and the liberal support of foreign capitalists, the Atlantic and Great Western, although a line of magnificent construction and equipment—second only to Erie, in fact—went steadily down until it was reserved for Messrs. Fisk and Gould to rescue it from bankruptcy and impending ruin, as they had previously rescued Erie, and make it one of the connecting links in the all-circling chain which their fertile brains have patterned, and which they have determined to devote all their vast wealth and exhaustless energies and resources to create. The prospects of the Atlantic and Great Western were bright and flattering at first, but the anomalous position it held between competing roads cramped its growth, and, not receiving the support of any great arterial line of communication, its business finally dwindled to a deplorable extent. Its history is not alone curious but instructive, as illustrative of the fate which is sure to overtake any enterprise started in opposition to the natural laws of commerce. The Atlantic and Great Western road can only be rendered a success by a union with Erie—a union under one management, with identity of interests and co-operation of capital and influence. Far-seeing and full of enterprise as they are, Fisk and Gould readily comprehended the necessities of the Atlantic and Great Western, and bent their energies to the work of accomplishing the desired consolidation. It needs no stretch of imagination to realize that when these two roads are as one, stretching from the great port of New York to the central waters of the Ohio, Erie stock will rise with a calm and steady and well-warranted persistency above all other stocks in the market. Look at the map and say if this is not an inevitable consequence.

THE EASTERN DIVISION.

Take the first, or Eastern Division of the Erie road, and follow the line of its broad-gauge, steel-railed, double track, past busy Paterson, and other of the more important and populous cities of New Jersey, thence through the heart of the rich farm lands of far-famed Orange

County, connecting a thickly dotted line of thriving towns and growing cities, such as Turner's, Munroe, Greycourt, Chester, Goshen, Middletown, Otisville and Port Jervis. At the last-named point, which is the terminal station of the Eastern Division of the line, the Company has located extensive machine-shops, car-shops and other works. At Port Jervis the Erie commences to freight its trains with the precious produce of the vast coal fields of Pennsylvania, and consequently the earnings of this division, with its immense local traffic, profitable connections, and tributary branches, are enormously large.

The Newburgh branch, extending from Greycourt Junction to Newburgh, on the Hudson, affords an outlet to tide-water for immense quantities of anthracite coal, which is transhipped to various ports of the United States. The Boston, Hartford, and Erie Railway, terminating at Fishkill, opposite Newburgh, connects with Boston, passing through numerous thriving manufacturing towns, and branches to Providence. From the important cities above named, lines radiate to every portion of New England and the Dominion of Canada. The Warwick Valley Road, extending from Greycourt to Warwick, is operated by the Erie Company. The branch from Suffern to Piermont on the Hudson, is eighteen miles in length. An immense pier, one mile in length, runs out into the river at the terminus of the line, and extensive freight-houses, engine-houses, and workshops are located at this point.

THE DELAWARE DIVISION.

The Delaware division extends from Port Jervis to Summit station. The scenery along this section is beautiful in the extreme. Three miles beyond Port Jervis the line crosses the Delaware River over a wooden bridge 800 feet in length, and for the next 26 miles runs on the soil of Pennsylvania. The Erie Company pays to the Quaker State $10,000 per year for the privilege of running their road on this side of the river, but in consideration of that sum is exempt from further taxation. Leaving Pond Eddy the road runs for a long distance along the steep and rugged bank of the Delaware—occasionally passing along the edge of some tremendous precipice. The most timid passenger need not be alarmed while in transit over these seemingly dangerous points, however, for every precaution is taken against accident. This portion of the road was extremely difficult and expensive to construct, being hewn through solid rock. In making the surveys for this portion of the line, the engineers had to be lowered down the almost perpendicular sides with ropes. The Hawley branch, which connects with the Erie main line at Lackawaxen, carries over a million tons of coal annually from the mines of the Pennsylvania Coal Company to Newburgh, Piermont, and Jersey City. Hancock, one of the most western stations of this division, is destined to be a place of considerable importance, it being the railroad outlet for the entire valley of the East Delaware branch.

THE SUSQUEHANNA DIVISION.

The Susquehanna division, which terminates at Hornellsville, three hundred and thirty-two miles from New York, embraces about one-third the distance between this city and Buffalo. It is under the superintendence of Mr. H. D. V. Pratt, a gentleman who has been connected with the road for over twenty years. The business of this section is really immense, and the fact that no accident of a serious nature has ever occurred on it is sufficient evidence of the satisfactory manner in which it is worked. The local business of the Susquehanna division pays the expenses of the road three times over. This section connects with the Delaware, Lackawanna and Western at Great Bend, and the trains of that line carry coal along the Erie track to Binghamton. They also run one or two trains per day to Owego and Ithaca. At Binghamton the Syracuse and Binghamton road, controlled by the Delaware and Lackawanna, and the Albany and Susquehanna lines connect with Erie. At Owego, the Owego and Ithaca connects, as also the Southern Central, running from Owego to Auburn. The Lehigh Valley road connects at Waverly, and brings the Erie an immense business in the way of coal, iron, and merchandise from Philadelphia, receiving as return freight grain and other products of the West. The Lehigh Valley line runs in direct and damaging competition with the Northern Central. Two new lines now in the course of construction will also connect with the Erie at Waverly—a line of forty miles from Ithaca, and a line of about twenty connecting with the Southern Central. Both will be completed some time next summer, and, as tributaries of Erie, will monopolize the immense business of the great coal fields of the Lehigh Valley, Towanda, and Fall Creek. The Northern Central road, running trains direct from Harrisburg, Philadelphia, Baltimore, and Washington, connects at Elmira, as also the Chemung branch. The Tioga road, which in the summer season brings in about 5,000 tons of bituminous coal per day, joins at Corning, and last there is the line from Corning to Rochester, with the Branch from Avon to Attica, of which the Erie Company has a perpetual lease.

At Waverly the Erie Company has a branch line extending to the Towanda mines, thirty-four miles distant, from which source is drawn all the coal consumed by the Erie line, along its entire length. No other line in the country is so advantageously provided for in this respect, an enormous saving being effected by supplying trains with coal fresh from the mines. The town of Waverly owes its importance in a great measure to the fact of its being one of the principal coal depots of the Erie road. The "pockets" erected by the Company at this point are capable of containing 14,000 tons of bituminous coal, and an equal quantity of anthracite. The former quality comes from Towanda, and the latter chiefly from Pittston and Lehigh Valley. Under the present management the station buildings are being extended, additional tracks laid, and the most modern and improved appliances for handling coal, loading locomotives, &c., have been erected.

VAST IMPROVEMENTS.

Twelve years ago the number of cars passing Susquehanna station, bound east, averaged but 2,412 per month. The average of the last ten months is 7,778—the bulk of the freight being grain, flour, and stock. Twelve years ago the sale of tickets at this point amounted to $300 or $400 per month, and about $600 or $700 was received for freight. Ticket sales now amount to $2,000 per month, and about $5,000 is collected for freight. It is estimated that the population of the towns and cities along the Erie road has more than doubled within the last ten years, and the probabilities are that within the next ten years a much larger increase will take place. Competent authorities at Susquehanna and elsewhere declare that the business of the line has largely increased since Messrs. Gould and Fisk assumed control, and the impression generally prevails that the present managers are by far the most efficient men ever in charge of Erie. Owing to Fisk's enterprise and Gould's careful nursing, it appears that the local business of the road has been doubled along its entire length.

Principal among the important improvements and extensions now being made in the neighborhood of Susquehanna, is a branch road from Carbondale to Lanesborough, connecting with Erie at the latter point. The object of this extension is to carry the coal from the mines at Carbondale to the Western markets. The new line will be thirty-five miles in length. About twelve hundred men are now engaged upon it. The work of laying rails will be commenced by May, and July will probably find the line in running order. The track follows the Lackawanna about half way from Carbondale, and then follows the course of the Starrucca Creek. Its profitable working is already assured—the Delaware and Hudson Canal Company have ing agreed to ship at the rate of 750,000 tons of coal per year over it—coal which is now being forwarded by the longer and proportionately expensive route of the Delaware, Lackawanna and Western line. This is only one of the numerous extensions projected by the genius and enterprise of Messrs. Fisk and Gould for the purpose of increasing the earnings of the Erie road—but this one alone adds $3,000,000 to the yearly revenues. The present management have determined on accomplishing, as soon as possible, two vast improvements, which, even in the absence of its other advantages, will render the Erie line first among the railroads of the future. Steel rails are to be substituted for iron, from one end of Erie to the other, and massive iron bridges are to span the waters now crossed by wooden frames, which are liable to be swept away by every freshet. Already some 180 miles of steel rails have been laid, and this work is being rapidly proceeded with. From New York to Susquehanna the rails are nearly all steel. One of the new iron bridges is now being thrown across the Susquehanna river, a short distance beyond the station. The bridge was constructed at Paterson, from the plans furnished by S. S. Post, civil engineer of Jersey City—a gentleman who has the reputation of being one of the most experienced bridge builders in the country. A mile or so on this side of Susquehanna is the Starrucca viaduct, one of the great wonders of American engineering. This magnificent and costly structure is 1,200 feet in length, 110 feet in height, and has eighteen arches. The span of the central arch is somewhere near 100 feet. Viewed from the valley below, the appearance of this massive yet graceful structure is imposing in the extreme. Some idea of the difficulties surmounted by the engineers of the Erie road may be formed on considering the following points : Twenty-six miles on the east of Susquehanna is Deposit, a station some 997 feet above the level of the sea ; between Deposit and Susquehanna is Summit, which is exactly 1,366 feet above the level—a difference of 369 feet in eight miles. From Summit to Susquehanna the road descends at a grade of fully 60 feet to the mile for a distance of eight miles. Six or seven heavy engines are kept on either side of Summit for the purpose of acting as "pushes."

SUSQUEHANNA AS AN ERIE DEPOT.

The picturesque and prosperous town of Susquehanna is one vast Erie depot. Of its population of 5,000, nearly all are dependant on the road. Twenty-two years ago the site of Susquehanna was a wild forest, but in 1848 the spot was selected as a central point, and the Erie Company purchased about 300 acres, and levelling a space by the side of the river, erected repair shops and other necessary buildings. No better location could have been chosen. The town has grown with the business of the road, and the greater portion of the 300 acres is now owned by the employes of the company, $375,000 having been realized so far by the sale of lots. The station buildings are handsome and commodious, and the company's hotel is a first-class institution, its accommodations comparing favorably with the best metropolitan establishments. The shops connected with the road form a considerable town by themselves, covering over six acres of land and employing about 600 men. They are under the immediate superintendence of Mr. J. B. Gregg, who has been connected with them since 1851. The machine or main shop is the largest of these structures, being 774 feet by 138—probably the largest building of its kind in the world, but certainly one of the best appointed and arranged. The centre aisle of this vast temple of industry is lined with locomotives—some just built, and others being repaired and reconstructed. Here is a spick-span new one, glittering with polished brass, and gorgeous with paint, snorting impatiently as it is driven out for its first trip on the road, and there is a worn-out iron-horse, being dragged on to the traverse table, which is used as an ambulance for disabled locomotives to be taken down to the other end of the shop and broken up. Looking down the long avenue of lathes with their interlacing bands humming so smoothly and rapidly over the whirring wheels, and listening to the tremendous "thuds" of the ponderous steam-hammers, the ringing blows which the muscular sons of Vulcan are showering upon their sounding anvils, and the deafening rattle of boiler-makers, who are busy, like Shakespeare's armorers, "closing rivets up," the visitor to these shops realizes in a measure the vastness of the business, and the wealth, power and importance of the corporation which built the town of Susquehanna for a division depot. The under-mentioned buildings adjoin the machine department: Boiler shop, measuring 200 feet by 116; blacksmith's shop, 180 feet by

86; carpenter's shop, 120 by 70; pattern shop, 120 by 70; paint shop, 120 by 60; pattern store-room, 120 by 60 coppersmith's, tin, and sheet-iron shop, 120 by 50; store-room, 120 by 50; foundry, 200 by 62; cleaning room, 85 by 40; sand rooms, 100 by 25; engine-room for foundry, 35 by 20; engine-room for shops, 85 by 25; and the hammer shop, which contains several steam-hammers, the heaviest being a 2,200-pounder.

In the semi-circular engine house, from which the different tracts connecting with the depot lines diverge, forty first-class locomotives repose, each in its separate stall. This is the stable for such of the iron horses of the unequalled Erie stud as are kept in reserve. Adjoining this building are handsome quarters occupied by the engineers of the station. At the rear is the gas manufactory, from which the whole of this extensive range of shops is lighted. The superintendent's office adjoins and overlooks the main machine shop, and attached to the offices is a large library of well-selected works, and a magnificent lecture-hall, capable of seating 600, provided for the use of the employes of the company. Some further idea of the extent of these works may be formed when it is stated that the steam-pipes which heat the different departments measure altogether something over ninety miles. A magnificent Corliss engine of 100-horse power, drives the machinery of the shops and gives motion to the line of shafting attached to the lathes. A fire engine of 100 lbs. pressure is kept going night and day, ready and equal for any emergency. The capacities of these works—enormous as they are—require frequent extensions to enable them to meet the daily increasing requirements of the road. The machinery employed throughout is of the most modern and approved pattern. The company's hotel, known as the Starrucca House, forms the center of the long range of station-buildings. The dining hall is a magnificently appointed appartment, 120 feet by 40, and lofty in proportion. The meals furnished here, as at the other establishments along the line provided by the company for the express accommodation of their passengers, are vastly superior to the "refreshments" supplied along other lines, and ample time is allowed for their dispatch. In this important particular the Erie managers have effected wonderful improvements, and are entitled to the gratitude of the travelling public. Why do the managers of rival lines—the New York Central and the Pennsylvania Central, for instance—not endeavor to compete with Erie in this respect?

ERIE WORKS AT ELMIRA.

At Elmira the Erie Company has some extensive works, principal among which are the car shops, which are superior in some particulars to the kindred establishments located at Jersey City, Port Jervis, and Buffalo. The work performed at Elmira is mainly of the better class. The magnificent drawing-room coaches and luxurious sleeping cars of the Erie line, which so far surpass those of any other road in the country, are mostly built at the Elmira shops, as also the superb first-class carriages now in use. The machinery of the Erie car shops is marvellously complete—performing almost everything but the joining and upholstery work. The greater portion of the elaborate carvings and costly ornamental wood-work which decorates the palatial drawing-room coaches is, of course, the result of artistic handiwork. Fresco artists of rare ability are employed to gild and fret the roofs with rich designs, and landscapists of considerable genius enrich the panels and fixtures with charming little bits of picturesque scenery. Occasionally fruit, flower, and even figure pieces enliven the interiors, and transform the drawing-room coaches into ambulatory art galleries. Of the men employed in the Elmira shops, about 150 are skilled artisans of the first-class. Mr. Rutter, the superintendent of the works, is engaged upon some new cars of his own design, which promise to be marvels of railway architecture, and will inevitably attract much additional traffic to the road.

THE BUFFALO AND NORTHWESTERN DIVISIONS.

The Buffalo division diverges from the main road at Corning, a large and rapidly growing town, situate in Steuben County, 291 miles from New York. Leaving Corning, the line of this division runs parallel with the main road for a short distance, and then diverges to the north, passing up the valley of the Cohocton River, through Steuben County, thence through Livingston County, between Conesus and Hemlock Lakes, to Avon, from which point a branch extends to Rochester. From Avon the route continues directly west through Batavia, in Genesee County to Buffalo. From Livonia, a station on the eastern border of the rich Genesee Valley, more grain is shipped than from any other point on the road. The most important station between Corning and Rochester is Avon, which is the center of one of the richest agricultural districts in the State of New York. From this point the Erie has two lines, one to Rochester, the other running west to Buffalo; and here the Genesee Valley road connects, and opens communications with Genesee and Mount Morris. Enormous quantities of grain, wool, fruit, and other farm produce are shipped from this locality. The Erie's connection with the flourishing City of Rochester results in tremendous additions to its revenues, making the grand total larger than the revenue of the government of the United States under Washington's administration.

The North-Western division diverges from the main line at Hornellsville, 332 miles from New York, and runs to Buffalo via Portage and Attica. The line crosses the Genesee river, in close vicinity to the famous Falls, over one of the largest wooden railroad bridges in the world. This wonderful structure stands upon thirteen massive stone piers, set in the bed of the river and rising sufficiently above high-water mark to be secure against freshets. The timber trestle-work supporting the track rises 234 feet above the piers. The bridge is 800 feet long and is so constructed that any timber in the whole structure can be removed and replaced at pleasure: it was built at a cost of $175,000. At Attica the Buffalo division of the Erie Railway, which diverges at Corning, as previously stated, re-unites with the North-Western division, forming a single line from this point to Buffalo, which city is twenty-five miles distant.

BUFFALO ERIE BUSINESS.

Mr. H. C. Fisk, the Superintendent of the Buffalo and North-Western divisions (who is, by the way, no relative of James Fisk, Jr.), speaks in glowing terms of the enterprise and ability of the present managers, and adduces much that is patent and irrefutable in support of his assertion that Messrs. Fisk and Gould have done more to extend the business and increase the earnings of the Erie road during the short time they have had the management of it than all the "old fogies" who preceded them put together could ever have accomplished, had they the brains to conceive such masterly plans and lives of patriarchal length to devote to their execution. And Mr. H. C. Fisk must be allowed to be somewhat of an authority on this point, since he has been in the employ of the Erie Company for over fifteen years, and is thoroughly posted as to the affairs of the road.

Until Fisk and Gould assumed the reins, the depot and freight buildings at Buffalo were altogether inadequate to the requirements of the road at that important point; but Gould " came, saw," and, with the able assistance of the Admiral, soon " conquered" the many difficulties which had so long cramped the business of the Buffalo division. " There never was such a team as Gould and Fisk!" exclaimed one of the Erie veterans on being asked for his candid opinion of the present managers; " let Gould make his plan, and Fisk put his broad shoulders to the wheel, and the thing is done instanter." The old servants of the Erie, by whom all positions of responsibility are occupied, express the greatest surprise at the close attention Messrs. Fisk and Gould pay to the business and condition of the road—nothing of any importance escaping their notice; and say there is some satisfaction in working under men who can appreciate their services.

The Erie freight houses on the dock at Buffalo measure, respectively, 300 feet by 200, and 560 by 200, and are fitted with every convenience for the handling of goods. The arrangements for the shipment of coal are being rapidly extended to meet the constantly increasing requirements of the road. The company owns about 2,000 feet of dockage on the river, and contracts for the excavation of rock along the bank have been entered into, which, when fulfilled, will give 3,000 feet additional dock room, and a coal yard of about two acres. A double track connects with the Niagara elevator—the largest and best in the city; and the extensive elevator owned by the company is similarly provided. In this respect the Erie enjoys a great advantage over every other line. Among other important matters to which Mr. Gould has devoted special attention is the loading of grain in bulk, and under his able management this new feature has been developed until it adds about a million and a half per year to the earnings of the road. In this particular, the interests of the corporation have not been neglected, and there is abundant evidence of a like nature all along the line, to prove that Messrs Fisk and Gould have done, and are still doing, all that lies in their power to benefit the Erie road. An important addition has recently been made to the freight facilities in the shape of a transfer house 600 feet in length, attached to which is a platform measuring 800 feet, specially designed and constructed for the purpose of transfering grain in bulk. In connection with these conveniences, arrangements have been made with the Lake Shore and Michigan Southern, which result in very material additions to the Erie revenues—from 75 to 100 cars of additional freight being received per day. When all the improvements projected by Fisk and Gould shall have been completed the business of the Buffalo division will be about three times as extensive and fully four times as profitable as it was before they became a power in Erie. The additional car and machine shops erected at this point during the past summer are now in full blast. The new engine-house, 150 feet by 30, is fully as well appointed as the larger establishment at Susquehanna. One hundred and fifty skilled artisans are kept constantly at work in the Buffalo shops. The passenger depot at this station is by no means in keeping with the handsome and commodious structures the company have provided at other points, but plans for a new range of buildings have just been approved, and the work of construction will be pushed on with all possible speed. Much attention has recently been devoted to the improvement of facilities for lake shipments, and twenty-one first-class steamers are now engaged in the transport of Erie freight. Here, then, is another instance of the extraordinary enterprise and exhaustless energy of Fisk and Gould—another illustration of their far-seeing policy. Then, again, the agencies and connections they have established in the different villages, towns and cities along their line influence additional business from all the points now touched, and pave the way for future extensions.

HORNELLSVILLE TO DUNKIRK.

Hornellsville is 332 miles from New York and 128 from Dunkirk. Leaving the valley of the Canisteo River at this point the line now bends towards the south and commences ascending the Whitney Valley at a grade of about fifty feet to the mile. From Tip Top Summit Station, the highest point on the entire route, being 1,760 feet above tide water, the road descends on a grade of forty feet to the mile. At Genesee the trade of a large region of country, extending into Potter County, Pennsylvania, centres, this being the nearest railway station, and accessible by the deep valleys of the tributaries of the Genesee River. From this point the route changes abruptly to the northwest, running through picturesque valleys flanked by steep hills ranging from 700 to 1,000 feet. Belvidere, the lowest point of the Genesee Valley reached by the Erie Railway, has become the outlet for the business of the surrounding country. From Cuba Summit, which is 1,677 feet above tide-water, the road passes over the Allegany ridge, on the eastern side of which rills, rivulets and rivers flow towards the great lakes, and thence down the St. Lawrence to the Atlantic; while on the other side, only a few rods further west, the water-shed becomes tributary to the Allegany River, and passing down its devious course to the Ohio and Mississippi, finds its way to the Gulf of Mexico. From Olean, which is situate at the junction of Oil Creek and the Allegany River, a new branch of Erie will, at no distant day, extend into the Pennsylvania coal regions. The Bradford, Buffalo, and Pittsburg Railroad (Bradford branch) connects with the Erie at Carrollton, Cattaraugus County, and runs south about twenty-eight miles to the bituminous coal mines of McKean County, Pennsylvania. At the junction of Little Valley Creek with the Allegany River is Salamanca, the initial point of the Atlantic and Great Western Railway, which extends from this point through Pennsylvania and Ohio to Cincinnati. From this station the Erie runs northwardly, while the Atlantic and Great Western follows the course of the Allegany River. Leaving Little Valley, the Erie again strikes the Allegany water-crest. From Dayton, which is 1,595 feet above the sea-level, and 1,015 above that of Lake Erie, the road descends on a gentle grade until it reaches Dunkirk, its original western terminus.

DUNKIRK.

Dunkirk was selected as the western terminus of the Erie Railway on account of its fine harbor, which is the best between Buffalo and Cleveland. At this point the Erie Company has an extensive range of warehouses and a number of workshops.

THE PRESENT EQUIPMENT.

While showing the enormous increase of three and a quarter millions of dollars in the earnings of the road for

1869 over the total of the previous year, the present management has increased the equipment as under:

December 1*st*, 1868.		*December* 1*st*, 1869.	
Engines,	371	Engines,	448
Passenger Cars,	188	Passenger Cars,	225
Freight Cars,	6,200	Freight Cars,	8,748

The difference being 77 engines and 2,585 passenger and freight cars.

FOURTEEN MILLIONS ACCOUNTED FOR.

The following statement, which is compiled on information obtained from most reliable sources, shows the cost and magnitude of the extensions and improvements made by Messrs. Fisk and Gould:

Constructing the New York and Newburgh Railroad,	$500,000
Constructing the Paterson and Newark Railroad,	600,000
Cost of Cattle-yards at Weehawken,	900,000
Cost of Oil-yards and Elevators at Jersey City,	1,800,000
Cost of improvements at Jersey City—new Passenger and Freight Depots, &c.,	250,000
Constructing new anthracite coal road from Susquehanna to Carbondale, 40 miles,	1,200,000
Cost of new Machine and Car Shops at Buffalo,	50,000
Cost of improvements at Buffalo for coal and freight traffic,	200,000
Constructing Pockets, Shoots, and Tressels at Waverly for coal brought by the Lehigh Valley Railroad,	25,000
Cost of new Freight House at Binghamton,	6,000
Cost of additional equipment, Engines, and Freight and Passenger Cars,	2,500,000
Purchase of half share in Rolling Mill at Trenton,	250,000
Cost of Steel Rails,	1,920,000
Improvements at Honesdale to do the traffic for Delaware and Hudson Coal Company,	40,000
Carried forward,	$10,241,000

Brought forward, ...	$10,241,000
Cost of establishing Steamboat Lines running in connection with railway from Buffalo to Toledo, Detroit, and Chicago, ...	700,000
Coal mines to supply the line with cheap fuel, ...	450,000
Laying Double Track, ...	1,200,000
Advance to Atlantic and Great Western Railway Company, under lease securing control of the road	1,600,000
New Coal Pier at Weehawken for traffic of Penn. Coal Co.	78,000
Track to connect with same, and right of way, ...	20,000
Cost of new Oil Depot and real estate at Pen Horn..	192,000
Cost of new Iron Bridge at Susquehanna....	64,000
Total, ...	$14,545,000

The fourteen millions expended as per above statement, may be regarded as a dividend shared between the travelling public and the freight patrons of the Erie road.

THE RAILWAY OF THE FUTURE.

That there is a glorious future for Erie must be evident to all. Its great destiny is already manifest. The untold mineral wealth which lies buried in the Susquehanna hills will ere long freight its trains, and this traffic alone will make Erie a dividend-paying corporation. Coal is abundant along the entire line, and capital is all that is required to make certain sections of the adjacent country rival the Lackawanna Valley. Money, enterprise, and increasing population will in a few years hence open up the immense resources of Western New York, and a little later in the coming period of general wealth and prosperity the wharves of Buffalo, Dunkirk, and the other harbors of Lake Erie will be crowded with shipping, freighted with the produce of the North-West—copper, lead, and quicksilver from the Superior mines; lumber and grain from Minnesota, and products of various kinds from the country bordering Lake Michigan. Extended according to the grand design of the present managers, the Erie will soon draw off the thronging freights which crowd the wharves and docks of Cleveland. This is no fancy picture. The Union Pacific Railroad was an "impossible scheme" ten years ago. To-day it is a marvellous reality. But greatest prospect of all for the Erie road is that of controlling the carrying trade of the Mississippi Valley and the Pacific slope. Striking St. Louis, twenty miles below the junction of the Missouri with the Mississippi, the connection of the Erie Railway extending from Cincinnati, will draw off the produce of the States bordering on the two greatest western rivers. Over the Central Pacific Railroad, now being pushed forward to the Rocky Mountains, the great bulk of California trade will finally be carried, and the dream of uniting the opposite civilizations of the world—the hoary oriental with the young and vigorous occidental—will be realized by the completion and consolidation of the Erie, Atlantic and Pacific, the railway of the future. Where will Erie stock be then? Built in the face of such formidable natural obstacles as met its course at every step; continued as a double track from the blue Atlantic to the gleaming waters of Lake Erie; with whole towns owing their birth and prosperity to it; with millions upon millions of dollars expended in improving its road-bed and equipments, and with an army of 23,000 men in its employ, the Erie Railway is not destined to be ruined by speculators.

The fight for the possession of the Albany and Susquehanna Railroad suggests a few thoughts which are in perfect harmony with the foregoing predictions as to the destined greatness of Erie. United to the Erie at Binghamton, the Albany and Susquehanna will connect at Albany with the New England lines running through the manufacturing sections "down East." By following the line of the Atlantic and Great Western road to Cincinnati, it will be seen that direct communication can be had with the cotton-growing regions of Tennessee, Georgia, and Alabama, and that New England manufacturers can purchase on a plantation and ship cotton direct to their factories. By this route it will come far cheaper than via the Mississippi and New Orleans, and thence transhipping by sea to New York, breaking bulk again for transit per rail to its destination. Every year the quantity of cotton consumed by New England mills is increasing immensely, and if only five dollars a bale is saved by direct railway transportation, we can easily see a quarter million dollars economized in the course of a month or so. If any men can accomplish this great overland freight line they will earn a high niche in the commercial wing of the Temple of Fame. Messrs. Fisk and Gould have already shown their appreciation of the one great difficulty under which our producers, manufacturers, and merchants are at present laboring, viz: the absence of cheap and sufficient freight accommodation, and it remains to be seen whether they will succeed in bringing about the much-desired improvements. Full and fast freight trains are particularly needed, for the country is filling with astounding rapidity and its distant parts demand better means of communication. The traffic of the continent centers to New York, and this city is altogether inadequately supplied with lines of communication for the accommodation of the ever-increasing burden of trade that seeks its patronage. Of all the roads leading from this point, however, the Erie offers superior facilities for the present trade, and makes the greatest efforts to meet the requirements of the future.

HOW THE SECOND CHAPTER WAS RECEIVED.

[Commenting editorially on the contents of this second CHAPTER OF ERIE, the *World* of December 11, 1869, says:]

"*Audi alteram partem*, even on Erie matters. So many charges of fraud and corruption have of late been made against Messrs. Gould and Fisk—charges, too, which, with all the circumstance of detail, have attracted wide attention everywhere—that the *World*, true to its usual fairness and impartiality, gives the defendants a chance to be heard in public. Their case certainly is a strong one, and the plea set forth in their behalf certainly has the merit of novelty. Fisk and Gould virtually appeal from Wall street to the people; from stockholders and speculators to Erie passengers and railway travellers; from courts and juries to shippers of grain and merchandise generally, and ask, "Are these our enemies?" and console themselves with the idea that they are not. They then show the improvements made on their great highway—the depots, workshops, and other buildings erected for the better traffic of the road; and last, but not least, furnish a tabular statement of extraordinary expenses incurred for said improvements, which, they say, accounts for the $14,000,000 over which there has been so much hue and cry since the Ramsey suit was first instituted."

IF NOT TRUE, OPEN TO REFUTATION.

From the N. Y. Evening Post of January 13, 1870.

Mr. George Crouch tells the world in a little pamphlet, called " Another Chapter of Erie," that it has greatly mistaken the character and designs of Messrs. Gould and Fisk, and asserts that in all their dealings they have had a single eye to the interest of the travelling and freighting public, and to the ultimate glory and usefulness of the Erie Railway. Mr. Crouch's account is not as clear or terse as it might be, his style is not as effective as that of the writer who gave us the first "Chapter of Erie;" but we have read what he writes, and this is the sum of it:

He asserts that when Messrs. Gould and Fisk came into control of the road, they found an empty treausry, and an urgent need of money; that they have raised and spent fourteen millions of dollars in improving the road; that they have improved its discipline, administration, efficiency, economy and power of serving the public and earning money for its stockholders; that the road earned during the year ending last October, $18,790,905, against $14,376,872 during the previous year; that the line is now in a more efficient condition, and better managed for both public and stockholders than ever before; that "owing to Fisk's enterprise and Gould's careful nursing, the local business of the road has been doubled along its entire length"; that 180 miles of steel rails have been laid, and this work is rapidly going on; that new iron bridges are substituted for wooden ones, new depots have been built, new branch lines bought, new connections perfected, preparations made for loading grain at lake ports in bulk; and that whereas in December, 1868, the road owned 371 engines, 188 passenger cars, and 6,200 freight cars; a year later, or last month, it possessed 448 engines, 225 passenger cars, and 8,748 freight cars.

The stockholders, Mr. Crouch tells us, may settle their quarrel with Messrs. Fisk and Gould; but the public have only to ask how well they are served, and need not trouble themselves with the woes of the stockholders. To a certain extent this is true. A railroad company is, so far as the general public is concerned, a creature to serve it; and if it doee its work at a loss to the stockholders, so long as it does the work well, its managers may say that the public have no right to look into the ledgers of the Company. We will add, that if a body of stockholders become so careless of their property and rights as to suffer them to fall into the hands of persons whose management is adverse to their interests, that also is their business and not the public's.

But there must be limits to this general rule, and these limits are believed to have been transcended by Messrs. Fisk and Gould in some of their transactions. We have been told that Mr. Fisk has acounted for these acts, on the ground that he found himself dealing with men of no conscience or respect for right or justice; that he and Mr. Gould took part in a great game of grab, and naturally "went in to win;" and that those who complain most loudly are precisely those who would have most unscrupulously fleeced them, if they had the power or opportunity.

This is a cynical view of the great Erie war; but it has also an element of truth in it, and we will only say of it now, that in such a contest no honor is to be won, and that scrupulous men would keep out of it.

If the statements of this Second Chapter of Erie are true—and if not they are open to refutation—Messrs. Fisk and Gould seem at least to have acted upon a general and broad plan in their management of the Erie Railway. Their offences against public morality are not to be condoned by this; but at least they may expect, if they increase the usefulness of the great road which they control, to earn a reputation for ability, which has not, so far, been conceded to them. If they are satisfied with this, they are easily contented; public opinion deeply resents their reckless and unscrupulous methods, and will not easily forget, whatever ability they may display, that they have outraged the moral sense of the community.

To say " we are no worse than others of our class," is to say too little. Nothing of late has excited so much indignation and ridicule throughout the country as the so-called monument to Mr. Vanderbilt. The whole press of the United States, with not an exception, so far as we know, except two journals in this city, spoke with contempt and derision of that attempt to suborn fame. If any man of first-rate ability is content to win no higher esteem and no greater character in the community than has been achieved by such men as Drew and Vanderbilt, it must be said that his ambition is not lofty.

A TRIUMPHANT VINDICATION OF FISK AND GOULD.

From the Hudson County Democrat Jan. 21, 1870.

SOMETHING ABOUT THE ERIE ROAD.—There is no portion of the country more directly and, prospectively, more largely interested in the success and good management of the Erie Railway than Hudson County. Its great tide-water terminus is at our shore, numerous work shops for the manufacture and repair of its cars and running gear are in our midst, and the future wealth and commercial importance of our immediate locality must necessarily depend in a large degree upon the results of its business. Everything, therefore, which concerns the prosperity of this great artery of trade cannot be otherwise than interesting to our readers.

We have just perused with much pleasure, and received considerable instruction from a pamphlet entitled " Another Chapter of Erie, by George Crouch." It is evident that the author is well versed in his subject, and that he brings to his task not only ability, but a thorough appreciation thereof. The importance of the road, and the mighty advantages it has conferred, and the still greater ones it is destined to confer in the development of agriculture, the building up of towns and cities, the increase of commerce and the facilities of inter-communication throughout a vast line of country embracing the wealthiest portions of the American continent are depicted not only with fervid eloquence, but with fair and logical certainty of anticipation based upon indisputable facts. The statistics of the road, its past history, present condition, and future prospects are portrayed with clearness and accuracy, and many errors which have gotten into the press through influences selfish and adverse to the present management are exposed and refuted.

The author is evidently a warm admirer of the genius and ability of Messrs. Gould & Fisk, yet he speaks of them with entire frankness, and makes no effort at special pleading in regard to the numerous charges which have been preferred against them; his chief object seems to be the success of the road as a good national blessing, and in so far as Fisk & Gould have contributed to this end, they receive his commendation. Putting by all side issues and making no attempt to defend these gentlemen as "financiers and speculators" he regards them simply as the managers of the Erie Railway, illustrates their administration and gives a highly interesting account of the present condition as compared with the past of the road and its interests, which is in itself a triumphant vindication of Fisk & Gould upon the great issue of the prosperity of the work they have undertaken.

Mr. Crouch in the first place described graphically the miserable condition of affairs when Messrs. Gould and Fisk first assumed control of the road; he says, "they found its treasury empty, and its reputation ragged in the extreme," and quoting from a prior pamphlet which we have not seen, adds: "that Messrs. Fisk and Gould could not have regarded their empty treasury, just depleted to the extent of nine millions—trust funds misapplied by directors in the process of stock-gambling—without serious question as to their ability to save the road from bankruptcy." "But the road *was* saved from bankruptcy," he says, "and to-day there is abundant evidence to show that it is in a fair way of becoming, ere long, the most prosperous line in the country."

The advantages of the road are glowingly set forth, and the improvements which have been made under the present management are described with an accuracy of detail which implies a full knowledge of the subject. The laying of steel rails, the purchase of additional engines, the new connections, with important branch lines, and various improvements of a nature to enhance greatly the value of the property, as well as increase the public facilities, have been done under this energetic management, and cost money; Mr. Fisk says himself, that $14,000,000 have been expended on the road in increasing its business conveniences. To do all this it is acknowledged that stock has been pretty freely "watered," which may have seemed hard upon stockholders, and which was disastrous to speculators; but our author considers this as a minor evil in comparison with the public benefits accruing from the improved condition and facilities of the road. On this subject he says very naively: "Whatever complaints the Erie stockholders may have against Messrs. Fisk and Gould on account of stock manipulations, &c., are matters in which the travelling public, and the traders and manufacturers who freight the trains on this great national thoroughfare, have very little concern." He considers the morality of Wall street a distinct virtue peculiar to that locality, with which the outside public cannot be consistently called on to interfere, and that the charges preferred against Messrs. Fisk and

Gould about "watering stock," "gold cornering," "unlawful appropriation of funds," &c., are altogether irrelevant to the subject under consideration.

It is not with Fisk and Gould as financiers of Wall street that we have to do any more than our author, but with them as the managers of a great national work, in which capacity we think he has shown in his pamphlet, to which we shall recur again, that they have consolidated the interests, increased the facilities and added largely to the business of the Erie road, conducting it for the public benefit with great skill and ability, and if their projects in connection therewith seem vast and comprehensive, they are at the same time reasonable and likely to be accomplished in the hands of such men.

A VIGOROUS DEFENCE—MEETING EVERY CHARGE WITH FACTS AND FIGURES.

From the Boston Post, Feb. 7, 1870.

The defence of the Erie Railroad management is vigorously made by Mr. George Crouch, in a pamphlet statement of the actual condition of the affairs of that road. It is entitled "Another Chapter of Erie," and should certainly be read with care by those who perused the assault. This very plain statement meets every charge of arbitrary conduct, of waste, and self-enrichment on the part of Messrs. Fisk and Gould, with such facts and figures as go to relieve them of the allegations which hostile parties have rained down on their heads. One can obtain from this new "Chapter of Erie" some adequate conception of the grand purposes of these two railway managers, and realize in a great degree the extent and complication of plans that stretch to their results across an entire continent. The statement brings forward into proper publicity the condition of the road and its exchequer, showing how heavily it had lost at the hands of a preceding management, the urgent necessity for raising money, the success of the great enterprise of extricating the company from its embarrassments and newly equipping the road, providing steel rails, securing a broad gauge, and constructing large and powerful engines and elegant and commodious cars; and it furnishes the actual figures to prove the immense progress in its business, thus appealing from rival judges and critics to the public that receives the benefit. It is a very strong, if not a convincing, chapter that is presented.

The tens of thousands of passengers over the road, the increasing list of shippers of grain and merchandise, the towns and cities along its line which have doubled their population in the last ten years—these are the best evidences to adduce, if the object is to show that the road is in the way to a grand and permanent prosperity. Within the past year, we are told, seventy-seven engines and twenty-five hundred cars have been added to the rolling stock of the road. The increase in the earnings has been three and a quarter millions of dollars. And a tabulated statement is given, item with item, to explain the reason of the expenditure of fourteen million dollars, on which is based the main charge of extravagance and misappropriation against Messrs. Gould and Fisk. These gentlemen are resolved on proving themselves great, not in Wall street, but in managing an arterial continental line of railway. They possess proven capacity and courage, cool heads, and vigorous determination, and are likely to make their magnificent promises good if suffered to go forward with their enterprise to the end. Mr. James Fisk has not his superior for liberal planning and energetic execution, and is bound up, heart and mind, in this gigantic task of making complete the Erie, Atlantic and Pacific Railway.

THE EIGHTH ANNUAL REPORT

OF THE

ERIE RAILWAY COMPANY,

For the Year Ending September 30, 1869.

To the Stockholders of the Erie Railway Company:

So much has been written and said both for and against the present management of the Erie Railway, that I deem it proper, in presenting a summary of the business of the last fiscal year, to take the opportunity of giving to the Stockholders the following account of what has been accomplished in the way of improvement to their property and the establishment of a reliable and profitable business for the future.

It is something over a year since the present management came into power.

THE CONDITION OF THE ROAD

at that time was not such as to attract the confidence of the traveling public, nor of the shippers of the products of Eastern manufactories and of importers to the Western States, and of the products of the West to the Eastern markets. The iron used in the track had been of an inferior quality, and was much of it worn out and unsafe: this, coupled with the accident at Carr's Rock the previous Spring, was injuring the business of the road, both passenger and freight, to such an extent that I felt it my duty to adopt the most effective measures at once.

By careful inquiry into the experience of European Railways in the use of

STEEL RAILS,

and of the operations of a few tons that had been laid on this Railway the previous year, I fully satisfied myself as to their great durability and strength, and of the necessity of our using them on the Eastern portion of the road where the very heavy traffic and the nature of the roadbed operates so disastrously to the iron rails. We have laid on the Eastern and Delaware Divisions nearly one hundred miles of solid steel rails—ten miles of American manufacture and the remainder procured from the best experienced manufacturers of England. The very great first cost of these solid steel rails—being more than twice the cost of iron rails—constrained me to investigate whether a middle course could not be adopted with advantage and economy: and while on the subject I was brought in communication with Mr. Abram S. Hewitt, of the firm of Cooper & Hewitt, who had just returned from Europe, where he went as one of the U. S. Commissioners to the "Exposition Universelle," and was then preparing to manufacture at the

TRENTON MILL, STEEL-HEADED RAILS.

While in Europe Mr. Hewitt had superior facilities for the investigation on the subject of steel-headed rails at the various places of manufacture as regards the process, and at the places where they were used as regards their service, and their relative value as compared with iron and with solid steel rails, and I availed myself of the favorable opportunity to secure the advantages to be derived from his valuable information and experience by making a contract with his firm, by which we became joint owners with them in the Trenton Mill, where, during the past year, they have been rolling these rails for us, in all about twelve thousand tons, or one hundred and twenty miles, and so far the results of their wear are eminently satisfactory. We have laid in all during the past year, including the steel and steel-headed rails, about four hundred miles of new track. The present condition of our track is equal if not superior to any in the country, and the reputation of the road in this respect is fully established as is fully demonstrated by our large and constantly increasing passenger traffic. By December 31, 1870, we hope to get the Eastern and Delaware Divisions, which have the heavy coal traffic of the Pennsylvania Coal Co. and the Delaware and Hudson Canal Co., entirely relaid with steel, which, though of greater cost in the first instance, is safest and cheapest in end, and will enable us to largely reduce the expenses of keeping up our track.

IRON BRIDGES.

My attention at the same time has been called to the matter of the bridges, which, being of wood, require frequent renewals, and the increasing scarcity of suitable timber along our line enhances their cost from year to year, and we have concluded to adopt iron bridges for all future renewals where the proper foundations for permanent piers and abutments can be obtained.

During the past season, in addition to several small bridges, we have had built an iron bridge 650 feet long—4 spans—for the crossing of the Susquehanna River, just West of Susquehanna Depot, which is now being placed in position.

With steel rails and iron bridges for a permanent way, we can safely predict large reduction of expenses, even with an increasing business.

LOCOMOTIVES.

The present management found the Locomotive equipment in a very worn and unserviceable condition, many of the engines having been run for years and maintained by patching, so that a large proportion required new boilers and fire-boxes, and many, entire rebuilding—the old machines being worth only the old scrap, but standing on the books and records of the Company as so many engines. These old engines have received the necessary attention as fast as possible for our shops to take them in, and they have been overhauled, and entire new engines in many cases turned out, with the same designating number, the whole expense being charged to repairs.

As additional equipment we have purchased from Paterson Locomotive Manufactories fifty new engines, ten of which have yet to be delivered on present contracts, and they are coming along at the rate of about four per week.

PASSENGER TRAFFIC.

During the fiscal year ending September 30th,

	1869.	1868.
Number of passengers carried in cars, - - - - -	2,497,113.	2,194,348.
Number of passengers carried one mile, - - -	128,445,158.	124,312,884.
Earnings from passengers,	$4,043,048,82.	$3,531,503.88.

To accommodate the increasing passenger business of the road, and also to keep pace with our competitors, we are rapidly replacing our old passenger equipment by new coaches of the best approved style of construction. We are also adding Palace or Drawing-room Coaches to our day trains, and have found them to be a popular feature of the road.

FREIGHT TRAFFIC.

	1869.	1868.
Number of tons of freight carried in cars, - - -	4,312,209.	3,908,243.
Total number of tons carried one mile, - - - -	817,829,190.	595,699,225.
Revenue from frieght,	$12,583,793.73.	$10,780,975.66.

To accommodate this large business we have made extensive additions to our equipment and endeavored to keep up to the wants and requirements of our local business as well as the through business. A very important feature of our freight business is the

COAL TRAFFIC.

The Erie Railway will, I hope, in a short time, become one of the most important coal carrying roads in the country. This business is very desirable—it is given to us in full trains and the rates are good.

During the year we have renewed the contract with the Pennsylvania Coal Company and increased the quantity to be transported for them annually from 900,000 to 1,200,000 tons, commencing December 1, 1869.

We have also concluded a contract with the Lehigh and Susquehanna Coal Company for a period of twenty years, with a gradually increasing tonnage commencing at 150,000 and running up to 500,000 tons annually from Honesdale to New York.

Under the present management this Company has obtained control, by a perpetual lease, of the Jefferson Railroad, extending from Hawley to Honesdale, where it connects the Erie system of roads with those of the Delaware and Hudson Canal Company. This road was completed and opened for coal traffic in Januaray last, since which time we have received from that Company a large and constantly increasing business. We are now loading at Honesdale from 200 to 300 cars per day. I estimate that in the year 1870 we ought to take from two millions to two millions five hundred thousand tons of anthracite coal from Hawley and Honesdale to tide-water. We certainly can do so if we can provide the cars and engines, and I hope not to default on that account.

Early in my connection with this Company I became convinced, that from the geographical position of our road and the many advantages offered by it to that end, it should do the carrying of the largest part of the anthracite coal consumed in the Western part of this State, as well as that sent to the Western States by the Lakes. On assuming the Presidency of the Company I at once commenced action to secure that trade, which I considered so very desirable, as it would be reliable, constant and increasing, and the haul would be long and the revenue large. Negotiations were opened with the Delaware, Lackawanna and Western Railroad Company, whose road connects with ours at Great Bend, and the terms of contract to run a number of years, for the transportation of a large amount of coal to Buffalo, a distance of 222 miles, were all agreed upon. And, though the agreement was not executed, negotiations had proceeded so far that shipments were commenced, and we had constructed more than one hundred cars of the large number we were to build and mark "D. L. & W." for that line, when that Company concluded an arrangement with the Syracuse and Binghamton Railroad, and the agreement with us was not executed nor carried out.

It then became necessary for us, in order to secure any of this trade, and assume the position to which we are entitled by reason of our line, to form some other connection, and to tap the very heart of the coal region. Negotiations were accordingly opened with the

DELAWARE AND HUDSON CANAL CO.

which, for the magnificence of its coal estate and the magnitude of its annual production, stands first among all the anthracite coal companies of the country, and an arrangement was made with them by which we agreed to construct a

RAILROAD FROM CARBONDALE TO SUSQUEHANNA,

a distance of forty miles, over which and thence 231 miles further on our main line to Buffalo, they are to ship annually a large amount of coal, commencing at 150,000 and running up to at least 500,000 tons by 1873, at favorable and remunerative rates. To make up for the time lost in the fruitless negotiations with the Delaware, Lackawanna and Western Railroad, the construction of this road has been pushed forward with all possible dispatch and will be completed before the next summer months. By this Carbondale road we have the shortest line from the anthracite coal fields to Central and Western New York and the Lakes.

THE LEHIGH VALLEY RAILROAD

having been extended, to form a connection with us at Waverly, gives us another coal-traffic feeder from which we are already receiving an average of about seventy-five car loads of coal per day. The coal from this road, at present, is loaded in our returning freight cars which would otherwise go through to Buffalo, 167 miles, empty. The time is but short when this Waverly connection will be of very great importance to us as a connection for coal and other freight.

PAVONIA FERRY.

We found the Pavonia Ferry running from the foot of Chamber steet, New York, to the passenger depot at Long Dock, Jersey City, for the accommodation of the passengers by our trains and the few people living near Pavonia Avenue in Jersey City. We constructed the ferry-houses and slips at 23d street, New York, and built two large, fine boats to run on that line. By this new line of ferry we have established a new depot in New York convenient to all the up town hotels and residences.

To increase the travel over our ferry beyond the train passengers, we have loaned our substantial aid to the construction of a horse railroad through the streets of Jersey City to Hudson City. This street road already promises to be a very profitable investment—it has assisted in building up that part of Jersey City and Hudson City through which it runs, and has brought larger increase to the revenue of our ferry as it connects with other street roads in Jersey City, running thence to Hoboken and to Bergen: and it has been of further advantage to this Company, as it runs through our property on the hill, at Hudson City, over the tunnel, and has enchanced its value by making it more marketable and desirable.

To further increase the ferry revenue we made an equitable contract with the

NORTHERN RAILROAD OF NEW JERSEY,

then running their trains over the New Jersey Railroad to the Cortland Street Ferry, for operating their road, by which we brought their trains to our ferry. So far under that contract we have averaged for that road about eight hundred car loads of passengers per month each way over the ferry, all of which is new business, and the contract for operating the road, which has so far paid its way, must eventually be profitable of itself.

We have also made the same kind of an operating contract with the

HACKENSACK AND NEW YORK RAILROAD,

which has averaged about five hundred car loads of passengers each way per month for the ferry.

The quantity and character of our freighting business has expanded to such an extent as to prove the comparatively large property at Long Dock altogether inadequate for the purposes of the Company, and we have deemed it absolutely necessary to procure more.

PROPERTY FRONTING HUDSON RIVER.

We have purchased, at a cost of $1,600,000, the property of the Weehawken Docks Company, situated just north of Hoboken, of about sixty acres, giving a river frontage of two thousand feet, where we have constructed a large pier for the handling of coal in transferring it from cars to boats. This pier has the best working arrangements, and is one of the largest on the river—capable of handling about four hundred cars per day.

This property is also used as the depot for handling refined oil, in barrels, and crude oil, in bulk. We have also concluded arrangements for the construction here of a large and commodious grain elevator, which will be the means of very largely increasing our transportation of bulk grain, and facilitate the unloading and prompt return of grain cars, thus enabling us to get much more service out of them.

We have also purchased the "Gregory Farm," situated about two miles North of the Weehawken Docks, of eighty acres, giving a river frontage of sixteen hundred feet. Here we have established our depot for the unloading of Live Stock, and built larger and commodious barns and pens, affording all the facilities for making it a Live Stock Market. It is already very popular with the stock men and will undoubtedly become the Live Stock Market of this city. The river frontage of this property we have improved by the construction of a strong and substantial bulkhead the whole length, making it available and desirable for the erection of warehouses, abattoirs, or other similar structures and for a lumber depot.

Between the Weehawken Docks and the Stock Yards is the property of the Delaware and Hudson Canal Company where they have large facilities for unloading and storing coal transported over our road.

Access is had to this property over the road of the Hoboken Land and Improvement Company, running North from the East end of Bergen Tunnel to the Canal Company's property, thence over the Fort Lee Railroad. With both of these Companies we have fair and equitable arrangements for use of their tracks. So much of the Fort Lee Railroad as is completed was built by us, which enabled us to obtain much more favorable terms for its use to our Stock Yards.

AT LONG DOCK

we have built two new piers, for the accommodation of our freight business, and added to and improved the old piers. We have also built a new passenger depot on an enlarged plan, to enable us to provide accommodation for the trains of the Northern Railroad of New Jersey, and the Hackensack railroad, and we are now re-building and adding to the number of the ferry slips.

JERSEY CITY SHOPS.

We have commenced the construction of a large machine shop which we found to be necessary on account of our large additions to our motive power—the walls, of brick, were all up when Winter set in and stopped the work—soon as the Spring weather will admit we shall resume work, and hope to shortly after complete it, when we shall have one of the largest and best appointed shops in the country. We have also built an extensive car shop, where, in addition to our repairs of coaches and freight cars, we are now turning out twenty new coal cars per day. We are also building several new coaches, with all the modern improvements, at this shop.

AT PEN HORN

we have made extensive purchases of real estate for the handling of crude oil in bulk, as we found the hauling of tank oil cars east of the tunnel was considered as endangering property and increasing rates of insurance, while it was too valuable a traffic for us not to work for, and give it all necessary accommodations. The oil is conveyed from here in pipes to Weehawken, and is only pumped through as vessels may be there to take it. All of this property will be in demand in a few years for refineries and warehouses of various kinds, as it is accessible by vessels *via* the Hackensack River. Already one refinery has been established there with a capacity of twelve hundred barrels per week, all the oil for which is transported over our road.

THE PATERSON AND NEWARK RAILROAD

which connects with us at Paterson was built with our aid, and we have entered into a contract with that Company for operating the road.

We found this railroad being constructed with a narrow gauge, and intended to connect at Newark with the narrow gauge roads running thence in connection with the Pennsylvannia roads for the West, and they were also promising to make such connections as would enable them to compete with us for passengers and freight between Newark and Paterson. Rather than allow a rival to reach the carrying business of our line we concluded it would be better to control the instrument, and by making it of the Erie broad gauge, enable us to tap the business of the extensive manufactories of the City of Newark and compete with the other roads for Western trade from that point, and also extend the market for coal and lumber from our main line. By the charter of that Company they will construct their road from Newark to make another connection with us at the West end of the tunnel, and such extension will make the road a profitable one and bring a large business to our ferry.

THE NEWBURH AND NEW YORK RAILROAD

was constructed by us from the Junction near Greenwood to a point on the Newburgh Branch, five miles from Newburgh, a distance of 13 miles, thus giving us a direct line between New York and Newburgh (sixty-two miles), and enabling us to compete with the River and with the Hudson River Railroad for the Newburgh and Cornwall travel.

THE DOUBLE TRACK

has been extended by us by the construction of the second track on the Delaware Division from "Turnout" to "Mid daugh," nine miles, and from Hancock to Deposit, thirteen miles; and on the Susquehanna Division from Painted Post to Erwin, four miles, and from Canisteo to Hornellsville, four miles. In all we have completed and opened thirty miles of double track; besides which we have done a large amount of work for the second track on other parts of the Delaware Division, and have done the grading and masonry for second track on Buffalo Division from Lancaster to Buffalo, ten miles, which is now all ready for the ties and iron.

ADDITIONAL SIDE TRACK

have been put in on all parts of the road as rendered necessary by the increased number of trains. At Buffalo, alone within the past year, more than two miles have been laid; Jersey City, two miles; Millville, Waverly, Hornellsville, and Castile, about one mile each, and other stations in proportion.

AT BUFFALO

we have also erected a large and well appointed car shop for the construction and repairs of coaches and freight cars at that end of the road. We have also erected an engine house and machine shop at Rochester.

The improvements at other stations, in the way of new freight depots, &c., as at Binghamton and Hornellsville, have been commensurate with the business requirements.

The increase in the tonnage and mileage of trains has made a corresponding increase in the quantity of fuel consumed, which is one of the very important items of operating expenses. Considering that the use of wood as locomotive fuel, besides being more expensive in the first cost per mile run, requires a very large amount of capital invested all the time, to keep a year's supply of properly seasoned wood ahead, we concluded to change our locomotives to coal-burners as fast as possible, and but a comparative small number are now burning wood. We are now using about eighty-five thousand tons of anthracite coal and one hundred and fifty thousand tons of bituminous coal per year; and in order that this large amount shall be procured at the lowest possible price, we have for the bituminous coal secured the

BARCLAY RAILROAD AND TOWANDA COAL MINES.

The railroad runs from Towanda, Bradford County, Pennsylvania, twenty miles from Waverly by the extension of the Lehigh Valley Railroad, to the coal mines, a distance of sixteen miles, and the coal is delivered on our road at Waverly to the transportation department at cost—at the present writing this coal is costing us about four cents per mile run less than in former years for the same kind of fuel. We have also made a proportionately good arrangement for our supply of anthracite coal, and we confidently expect that future statements will show a large reduction in this item of our operating expenses.

GENERAL OFFICES, 23D STREET.

The old offices of the Company in Erie Buildings, West Street, were constructed nearly twenty years ago when the requirements of the road for office room for the accommodation of the officers and clerks were not one fourth of what the now are, and this old building had been so enlarged and altered over to meet the increased wants from time to time, that by many it was considered unsafe to make any more alterations to it. It had also arrived at that condition on account of its various changes, as to be incapable of being properly heated in winter, and the ventilation was so bad as to be destructive to the health of the many persons employed in it. We, therefore, considered it necessary to make a change, inasmuch as we required more room, and as there was no necessity of the offices being on the dock, we thought best to move up town, where it would be more convenient for all persons connected with the Company in going to and from their homes. The building where we now are was the only one large enough for the purpose that we could secure, and here we have arranged offices to suit the wants of the several departments; and in fitting them up it was considered the best economy to make them not only comfortable and convenient, but attractive for the many persons necessarily employed on the premises, as well as for the large number of officers of other railroads, and the business public, whom we have to receive from time to time.

The foregoing is a brief statement of the principal operations of the present management, on the line of the road; the object in all cases, as will clearly appear, has been for the permanent improvement and lasting benefit of the Company;—if mistakes have been made in any, time alone will show them. In my judgment they were all entered into on correct principles, and on reviewing the work at this time I am clearly of the opinion that it is but a few months before that fact will be clearly demonstrated to all.

Having treated so far of our domestic arrangements and policy, I have a few words to say in regard to our

FOREIGN RELATIONS.

When we assumed the management we found combinations being formed all around us, by the New York Central and the Pennsylvania Central Railroad Companies, which threatened to cut us off from all connections controlling any of the through business of the West and so leave us merely a local institution. Believing the capacity of this road to be such as to enable it to take care of its full share of the through traffic, and that it was the intention of the originators of this enterprise that it should be a National institution, and one of the main (if not the very principal) channels of commerce between the East and the far West, we considered that the good of the whole country as well as the interests of our Stockholders demanded of us that these combinations should be defeated. We therefore entered into the spirit of this contest, determined, if possible, that the Erie Railway should take its true position in the carrying trade of the country. Our first attention was called to the

ATLANTIC AND GREAT WESTERN RAILWAY,

which was built with a six feet gauge from Salamanca, N. Y., to Dayton, O., where it connects with the Cincinnati, Hamilton and Dayton Railroad, over which there is a track of the same guage to Cincinnati, connecting with the Ohio and Mississippi Railroad to Saint Louis, making a road of continuous six feet guage from New York to the Mississippi River, with a branch to Cleveland and another to the oil regions of Pennsylvania. The Atlantic and Great Western Railway had been built under the influence of the Erie Railway Company, who had for a term of years paid tribute to it in the way of extra allowances or commissions for the through freight and passengers brought to Salamanca, which extra allowances had amounted to more than half a million of dollars, and had been the means of enabling it to get through, but was then in the hands of a Receiver. It was in contemplation to take that road into the narrow guage system, and in the interest of the Pennsylvania Central Railroad, which would leave us only the necessary traffic between their local stations and the local stations of our road, when in December, 1868, we took possession under the terms of a lease to operate it for a per centage of the gross earnings. After we took possession and had advanced the necessary money to pay the obligations of the Receiver, which was a condition of the Court, it was found that under the then existing laws of the State of Ohio, the lease, so far as related to the operations of the road, was of no validity. We then had a bill placed before the Ohio Legislature amending the Statutes so as to remove the difficulties of the question raised, which was passed, when Mr. McHenry, who had a scheme for funding the past due interest on the bonds, and which he found likely to fall through, interposed objections and prevented ratifications of the lease under the amended law. The road then, necessarily, went again into the hands of Receivers. That lease was entered into by us in good faith, but we were unwilling to be a party to the payment of any money on it for the benefit of any one until the Bondholders were satisfied, otherwise there would be no permanency to the arrangement, as any unsatisfied Bondholder could break it and remove us from possession by obtaining the appointment of another Receiver.

Uncertainty, and litigation brought on by disappointed parties, followed; but the matter has now all been adjusted and we are again in possession and operating the road on substantially the same terms as of the original lease.

THE CINCINNATI, HAMILTON & DAYTON R. R. CO.

have made a contract with us, giving us the use of the broad gauge track over their road to Cincinnati, and of their depots and station accommodations at all their stations on very favorable terms, the expenses of the road being pro-rated according to the amount of business done on the broad and narrow tracks. We thus have control of a road to Cincinnati and to Cleveland, and by an arrangement with the

OHIO & MISSISSIPPI RAILROAD

for mutual exchange of business, have unbroken communication with St. Louis, and in a few weeks a broad gauge line will be open to Louisville.

We have also secured control of a majority of the Eastward business on Lake Erie, at Buffalo, by an arrangement with the

UNION STEAMBOAT COMPANY,

who, in season of navigation, run a line of twenty-two steamboats from that port.

At the same time our relations with the

LAKE SHORE AND MICHIGAN SOUTHERN RAILROAD

for exchange of business at Buffalo, Dunkirk and Cleveland are eminently satisfactory and secured by mutual understanding and agreement, so that business connections and relations are secured with all Western roads, and we are placed on the same footing with them in that respect as other trunk lines.

BOSTON, HARTFORD AND ERIE RAILROAD.

Prior to my becoming the Executive officer of the Company, the Board of Directors had voted to give the Boston, Hartford and Erie Railroad Company substantial aid in the shape of a purchase of $5,000,000 of their first mortgage bonds. Since I have been President, we have paid for and taken up the bonds. This road will be a very important connection, as it will open to us the heart of the manufacturing district of New England. It is expected that the line will be open for business during the year.

NARRAGANSETT STEAMSHIP COMPANY.

Our relations with New England have been further greatly improved and cemented during the past year by a close alliance with this popular line of finest inland steamers in the world, connecting us directly with Newport, Fall River, and Boston. Our bnsiness of cotton from Cincinnati, and the South-West, to Fall River, which has more spindles than any other manufacturing town in this country, is large and rapidly increasing.

Before closing this report I have a few words to say in regard to the so-called "Director's Bill," which was passed by the Legislature of this State last winter, providing for the classification of the Directors of several railway companies, and the election of but one-fifth of the whole board each year. This law was carefully considered in both branches of the State Legislature, and was passed with scarcely a dissenting vote. No action whatever was taken on it by the then existing Board of Directors of this Company—and they had a right to take advantage of it and extend their term of office—but it was left for the Stockholders themselves to say whether they would accept the law or not. At the annual election, last October, it was accepted without a dissenting voice, and the present Board was elected by over three hundred and fifty-five thousand votes. In my judgment this is a wise law, and will secure to the property a responsible, experienced, and intelligent management, and be the means of preventing in the future the sudden changes in the policy of this magnificent railway, peculiar to it in the past while it was a mere creature of Wall street speculation.

The litigation that has been forced on us from time to time has not been of our seeking. We have considered that we were put in charge of this great trust by the expressed choice and will of the Stockholders, and we considered it to be our duty to them after having accepted, to retain possession against any small minority, until the Stockholders themselves should express their pleasure for a change by the choice of another Board, and to manage the property as we might consider for the permanent good.

For details of the operating expenses, &c., of the year, I refer to the annexed statement, made in the form required by the Legislature.

JAY GOULD,
President.

OFFICE ERIE RAILWAY CO.
New York, January 17, 1870.

REPORT

Of the Erie Railway Company to the State Engineer and Surveyor of the State of New York, made pursuant to Chapter 140 of the Laws of 1850.

Being for the year ending September 30th, 1869.

STOCK AND DEBTS.

1.	The Capital Stock, as by Charter:	
2.	The Amount of Stock Subscribed,	$78,536,910 00
3.	The Amount paid in, as by last Report,	46,302,210 00
4.	The Total Amount now paid in of Capital Stock,	78,536,910 00
5.	The Funded Debt, as by last Report,	23,398,800 00
6.	The Total Amount now of Funded Debt,	23,398,800 00
7.	The Floating Debt, as by last Report,	4,893,735 81
8.	The Amount now of Floating Debt,	
9.	The Total Amount now of Funded and Floating Debt,	23,398,800 00
10.	The average rate, per annum, of Interest on Funded Debt,	7 per cent.

COST OF ROAD AND EQUIPMENT.

		By last report.	By present report.
11, 12.	For Graduation and Masonry,	$1,501,643 11	$2,309,125 47
13, 14.	Telegraph,	12,326 52	12,326 52
15, 16.	Superstructure, including iron,	2,179,724 20	3,274,894 79
17, 18.	Passenger and Freight Stations, Buildings and Fixtures,	849,536 34	881,182 93
19, 20.	Engine and Car-Houses, Machine Shops, Machinery and Fixtures,	1,580,516 21	1,784,018 47
	Carried forward,	$6,123,746 38	$8,261,548 18

	By last report.	By present report.
Brought forward,	$6,123,746 38	$8,261,548 18
21, 22. Land, Land Damages and Fences,	335,563 36	350,922 88
23, 24. Locomotives and Fixtures, and Snow Plows,	2,672,611 96	3,103,907 16
25, 26. Passenger & Baggage Cars,	694,818 17	847,908 15
27, 28. Freight and other Cars,	2,654,706 77	3,488,760 28
28½. Pavonia and 23d Street Ferries,	266,210 48	526,962 43
29. 30. N. Y. & Erie Railroad Company,	43,738,948 85	48,551,949 93
31. Total cost of road and equipment,	$56,486,605 97	$65,131,959 01

CHARACTERISTICS OF ROAD.

32. Length of road,	459 Miles.
33. Length of road laid,	459 "
34. Length of double track, including sidings,	380¾ "
35. Length of branches owned by the Company, laid,	364¼ "
36. Length of double track laid on same,	50½ "
37. Weight of rail, per yard, on main track,	64 @ 70 lbs.
38. Number of engine-houses and shops,	40
Number of engines,	404
Number of 1st class passenger cars (rated as 8-wheel cars),	213
Number of 2d class and emigrant passenger cars (rated at 8-wheel cars),	54
Number of baggage, mail and express cars (rated as 8-wheel cars),	71
Number of freight cars (rated as 8-wheel cars),	7,447

Length of main line of road from Jersey City to Dunkirk, 459 Miles.

DOINGS OF THE YEAR IN TRANSPORTATION, AND TOTAL MILES RUN.

40. Number of miles run by passenger trains,	2,837,407
41. Number of miles run by freight trains, --	4,924,172
43. Number of passengers (all classes) carried in cars, ----------	2,497,113
44. Number of miles traveled by passengers, or number of passengers carried one mile, ----------	128,455,158
45. Number of tons, of 2,000 pounds of freight carried in cars, ----------	4,312,209
46. Total movement of freight, or number of tons carried one mile, ----------	817,829,190
47. Average rate of speed adopted by ordinary passenger trains, including stops (miles per hour), ----------	20
48. Rate of speed of same, when in motion, -	26
49. Average rate of speed adopted by express trains, including stops, ----------	26 and 30
50. Rate of speed of same, when in motion, -	30 and 40
51. Average rate of speed adopted by freight trains, including stops, ----------	10
52. Rate of speed of same, when in motion, -	12
53. Average weight, in tons, of passenger trains, exclusive of passengers and baggage, ----------	150
54. Average weight, in tons, of freight trains, exclusive of freight, ----------	220

55. The amount of freight, specifying the quantity in tons:

Of the products of the forest, ----------	191,629
Of animals, ----------	273.548
Of vegetable food, ----------	322 978
Other agricultural products ----------	15,752
Manufactures, ----------	436,846
Merchandise, ----------	459.784
Other articles, ----------	2,611,672
Total, ----------	4,312,209

42. "The rate of fare for passengers, charged for the respective classes per mile," as follows:

	Cents.
For first class through passengers, ...	2.05
For first class way "	2.73
For second class through "	--
For second class way "	--
For emigrant through "	1.22
For emigrant way "	1.47

Expenses of Maintaining the Road or Real Estate of the Corporation.

	AMOUNT.	ALLOTTED TO	
		Passenger Transportation.	Freight Transportation.
56. Repairs of Road-bed and Railway, excepting cost of Iron, (see law)*..	$1,984,560 26	$535,831 27	$1,448,728 99
57. For depreciation of way,............	....	....	....
58. Cost of Iron used in repairs:........	1,559,122 50	420,963 08	1,138,159 42
Allotted to passenger transportation, length in feet,...1,017,691 weight in lbs.,..20,983,781			
Allotted to freight transportation, length in feet, ...2,751,535 weight in lbs., ...56,733,928			
59. Repairs of buildings,..............	322,983 61	87,205 57	235,778 04
60. Repairs of fences and gates, ...	48,111 91	12,990 22	35,121 69
61. Taxes on real estate,...............	333,495 08	90,043 87	243,451 21
62. Totals, ...	$4,248,273 36	$1,147,034 01	$3,101,239 35

* 56. "For repairs of road-bed and railway, excepting cost of iron, which shall be the cost of labor and materials used during the year; also use and cost of engines engaged in ballasting; also the renewal and repairs of gravel and stone cars, and all items of cost connected with keeping the road in order."

Expenses of Repairs of Machinery.

	AMOUNT.	ALLOTTED TO	
		Passenger Transportation.	Freight Transportation.
64. Repairs of engines and tenders,.....	$1,373,867 49	$401,931 40	$971,936 09
65. Depreciation of engines and tenders,	....	....	....
66. Repairs of passenger & baggage cars,	396,076 80	396,076 80	....
67. Depreciation of passenger and baggage cars,......................	....	....	....
68. Repairs of freight cars,............	1,144,675 14	....	1,144,675 14
69. Depreciation of freight cars, ...	....	....	....
70. Repairs of tools and machinery in shops,..........................	138,378 54	49,816 27	88,562 27
71. Incidental expenses, including oil, fuel, clerks, watchmen, &c., about shops, ...	129,636 10	46,669 00	82,967 10
72. Totals, ...	$3,182,634 07	$894,493 47	$2,288,140 60

EXPENSES OF OPERATING THE ROAD.

	AMOUNT.	ALLOTTED TO	
		Passenger Transportation.	Freight Transportation.
73. Office expenses, stationery, &c., ...	$251,080 14	$64,770 04	$186,310 10
74. Agents and clerks, ...	872,952 93	218,238 23	654,714 70
75. Labor: loading and unloading fr't.,	633,223 66	....	633,223 66
76. Porters, watchmen & switch tenders,	198,813 49	53,679 64	145,133 85
77. Wood and water station attendance,	27,692 51	7,496 98	20,195 53
78. Conductors, baggage and brakemen,	854,382 34	262,028 74	592,353 60
79. Enginemen and Firemen, ...	900,968 28	276,809 59	624,158 69
80. Fuel, cost & labor of prepar'g for use,	1,406,412 24	506,308 41	900,103 83
81. Oil and waste for engines & tenders,	165,197 79	50,249 24	114,948 55
82. Oil and waste for freight cars, ...	25,096 66	....	25,096 66
83. Oil and waste for passenger and baggage cars, ...	7,990 13	7,990 13	....
84. Loss and damage of goods & bag'ge,	141,543 45	38,216 73	103,326 72
85. Damage for injuries of persons, ...	67,547 49	67,547 49	....
86. Damage to property, including damages by fire & cattle killed on road,	10,194 41	2,752 49	7,441 92
87. General superintendence, ...	119,234 14	32,193 22	87,040 92
88. Contingencies, ...	146,029 52	39,427 97	106,601 55
89. Totals, ...	$5,828,359 18	$1,627,708 90	$4,200,650 28

90. The above statements are to be made without reference to the sums actually received or paid during the year.

EARNINGS AND CASH RECEIPTS AND PAYMENTS.

1st. Earnings.

91. From Passenger Trains, ...	$4,043,048 82
92. From Freight Trains, ...	12,583,793 73
93. From other sources, ...	94,657 79
Total, ...	$16,721,500 34

94. The above to be stated without reference to the amount actually collected.

2d. Receipts.

95. From Passengers, ...	$3,429,629 18
96. From Freight, ...	13,046,803 76
97. "From other sources—specifying what, in detail," as follows, viz.:	
Telegraph, ...	33,562 61
Storage, ...	3,740 14
Rents, ...	22,831 76
Mails, ...	150,409 61
Pavonia Ferry, ...	34,523 28
Total, ...	$16,721,500 34

3d. Payments other than for Construction.

98.	Transportation Expenses, ...	$13,259,266 61
	Hudson River Ferry, ...	184,514 15
	Telegraph, ...	107,273 59
99.	Internal Revenue Tax, ...	88,566 44
	Loss on Lake Erie Steamers, ...	78,464 64
		$13,718,085 43
100	Interest on Mortgage Debt, ...	1,703,773 00
	Rents of Railroads, ...	824,020 00
		$16,245,878 43
101	Surplus October 1st, 1869, ...	475,621 91
		$16,721,500 34

Accidents from October 1st, 1868, to September 30, 1869.

DATE.	Passengers.		Employes.		Others.		Total.	
	Killed.	Injured.	Killed.	Injured.	Killed.	Injured.	Killed.	Injured.
1868.								
October,..	..	2	2	8	2	..	4	10
November,	..	..	4	3	2	1	6	4
December,	..	..	3	5	2	1	5	6
1869.								
January, .	1	..	4	3	..	4	5	7
February,	..	6	3	6	1	..	4	12
March, ...	1	2	1	4	2	4	4	10
April, ...	..	..	3	6	1	1	4	7
May, ...	..	1	6	2	2	..	8	3
June, ...	1	2	..	8	1	5	2	15
July, ...	6	8	..	11	3	1	9	20
August, ..	1	..	5	6	3	2	9	8
September	..	1	9	6	6	5	15	12
Killed, ..	10	..	40	..	25	..	75	..
Injured, ..	..	22	..	68	..	24	..	114

(Signed) JAY GOULD, *President.*

(Signed) L. D. RUCKER, *General Superintendent.*

OPINIONS OF THE PRESS.

The impression created by the foregoing report, on the parties in interest and the public at large, has been of such a satisfactory nature as to determine the present management of Erie to pursue the same bold policy of reform and retrenchment with which they have achieved such marvelous results during the first year of their stormy but extraordinarily successful administration; and has given them the gratifying and stimulating assurance that at last there is a prospect of their services being recognized and appreciated by those who are destined to be most benefitted thereby, *viz.*:—the owners of the vast and magnificent property they have rescued from ruin by their indomitable energy and perseverance, and the travelers and traders who have profited so largely by their vigorous opposition to extortionate monopolists.

The following comments on Mr. Gould's report, selected almost at random from an embarrassingly extensive collection of equally favorable editorial reviews, will suffice to show how wrongfully the present management has been abused in the past, and how necessary it is for the interests of Erie and the maintenance of national credit at home and abroad that they should have fair play in the future.

"FLATTERING FOR THE FUTURE OF THE ROAD."

From the New York Herald, January 21, 1870.

THE ERIE RAILWAY—ANNUAL REPORT OF THE COMPANY TO THE STOCKHOLDERS.—The President of the Erie Railway has prepared on behalf of the Company an elaborate report of the operations of the road for the last fiscal year. We publish the report elsewhere in our columns this morning. Inasmuch as the public have loudly complained of the management of Erie affairs, the report of Mr. Gould is in a measure defensive of the policy which has been pursued by the company since the present direction came into power. The showing is certainly flattering for the future of the road, whatever has been the course of its management in the immediate past. The earnings have been increased nearly two and a-half millions during 1869 as compared with 1868, but the money has been expended in extensive improvements, the character of which is given in detail in the report; hence the absence of dividends. As the stockholders of Erie are legion, and comprise capitalists and private investors at home and abroad, the facts and figures as set forth in the report will be read with great interest.

"ADMIRABLE, SUCCESSFUL AND ECONOMICAL MANAGEMENT."

From the New York Tribune, January 21, 1870.

Alaska has a tropical climate, and strawberries in their season. The Borgia was a saintly, much-slandered, martyr of a woman. The Devil is white. Mr. Jay Gould shows how *admirable, successful and economical* is his management of the Erie Railway.—[*See Opinions on the Press, for Tribune article in extenso*].

A GRATIFYING EXHIBIT TO THE STOCKHOLDERS.

From the N. Y. Evening Telegram. Jan. 22, 1870.

A document scarcely less important, in many respects, than the recent Message of the President of the United States, or still later that of Governor Hoffman, is the report of Jay Gould, President of the Erie Railway Corporation, to the stockholders of the company. The immense interests involved in connection with this road, and the peculiar circumstances surrounding the present management, render this report of far more than ordinary interest, and bespeak for it an attentive consideration quite equal to either message above referred to. The one under consideration at present has the merit of brevity, *and is nothing more than a simple statement of what has been done by the present direction in Erie during the past year. The exhibit is certainly a gratifying one to the stockholders*, beginning with the laying of 400 miles of new track, including steel and steel headed rails, reciting further the building of an iron bridge, 650 feet long, four spans, over the Susquehanna river, and several small iron bridges, the repairing of all the old locomotives and the purchase of fifty new ones, and the establishment of machine shops at Jersey City and Buffalo—together with repair shops at various points along the line. The report contains likewise particulars of contracts entered into with numerous coal companies, and closer business connections made with various ferry and railroad companies and steamboat lines, as well as extensive purchases of real estate.

After reviewing fully, although succinctly, these proceedings so far as they relate to the "domestic policy" of the road, the report enters upon a review of the "foreign relations," showing the policy pursued in that connection to have been of the offensive-defensive kind *forced upon the road by the combinations of rival corporations.*

Referring to the progress making in the Boston, Hartford and Erie road, and incidentally puffing the Narragansett Steamship Company, this most interesting document winds up with a defense of the so-called "Directors' Bill."

"AN ACCURATE REPORT AND SATISFACTORY EXHIBIT."

From the Buffalo Commercial Advertiser, January 24, 1870.

On our first page will be found a full and elaborate report of the operations of the Erie Railway for the last fiscal year, signed by its President, Jay Gould, Esq. So much has been said against the present management of the Erie, on all sides, that we regard it as due to truth and justice to give them a full hearing; and it is in the interest of fair play, therefore, that we bespeak for the rather long but interesting document a careful and candid perusal by our readers.

We have no doubt whatever that the statistics given, and the description of the improvements made in the road, may be relied on as accurate; and certainly the facts constitute a most satisfactory exhibit of the condition, and warrant the most encouraging view of the future, of this great national thoroughfare. Say what you will of the stock-jobbing and legislative operations with which the management have been charged,—and we would certainly interpose no defence of such illegitimate practices,—the fact remains well established that under no previous management of the Erie have the details of its practical working, and the interest and comfort of the traveling community, been so conscientiously looked after as under the management of Mr. Gould; and the natural result of this is clearly shown in the great increase of business over the line, as demonstrated by the statistics given in the report. It appears, in brief, that the earnings have been increased nearly two and a-half millions during 1869 as compared with 1868, though the money has been expended in much-needed and extensive improvements.

"SHOWING GOOD RESULTS IN THE WAY OF PRESENT BUSINESS, AND FLATTERING PROSPECTS FOR THE FUTURE."

From the Buffalo Express, Jan. 24, 1870.

The just published report of the President of the Erie Railway Company, Jay Gould, makes a more favorable exhibit of the management and business of that road during the past year than the public has had reason to expect. * * * *

[*Here follow extracts from the report.*]

Much of the report is given to a detailed account of the negotiations and arrangements by which a new extensive and prospectively immense coal traffic is secured for the road.

Into the long details which the report gives of the "foreign relations" established by the company, looking to far-reaching Western combinations, we cannot enter. The whole exhibit of management, as we have said is favorable, and shows both sagacity and energy of policy, with good results of present business and flattering prospects for the future. If, along with the shrewd, indomitable energy which unquestionably characterizes the Gould management, there could only be more scrupulousness of measures the affairs of the Erie Railway would seem to be in capable hands.

AN UNEXPECTEDLY GRATIFYING EXHIBIT.

From the Cleveland Leader, Jan. 24, 1870.

In solemn contradiction of all that has been said and written against the managers of the Erie Railway, there comes from the Opera Building in New York the long and glowing report of President Jay Gould, setting forth the past management and the present condition of the road. To the public generally, and to the patient stockholders of that corporation in particular, the report in question will be a surprising and unexpected piece of reading. According to this report, the Erie Railway is now in the full tide of success. Mr. Gould sets forth, that upon taking charge of the road, something over a year ago, he found the machinery, the buildings and the roadway in a most deplorable condition. The iron composing the track had been of a cheap, inferior English grade; many of the rails had broken down after only a few weeks' use, and the deplorable disaster at Carr's Rock during the preceding spring had made the very name of "Erie" a terror to travelers. Under these trying conditions, his earnest and constant purpose has been to put the road and its equipment into thorough working condition. Worn-out engines have been rebuilt or replaced by new ones, many thousand new cars have been added to the machinery of the Company, and almost the entire track relaid with either steel or the best grade of iron rails. New and advantageous combinations have been made for developing and fostering the traffic in coal, oil and the other leading products along the line; branch roads have been leased and made subsidiary to the Erie interest, and valuable property purchased and adapted to the needs of the Company in New York city, Buffalo and various points along the line. Mr. Gould takes up *seriatim* all important expenditures, and explains upon what grounds the outlay was deemed necessary. In the matter of earnings, the report makes an unexpectedly gratifying exhibit.

After reading this statement, the first and most natural question that will occur to the stockholders is, why so prosperous a company should not enjoy the luxury of an occasional dividend. This is a question which the Erie management has doubtless often been asked before, and it is the avowed purpose of the report to set all such questions definitely at rest. It is not so much an official report of the usual type as it is an explanation by Mr. Gould as to where the money goes. It must be admitted that the Erie President makes his point. He shows the road and its equipment to have been, at first, in an almost totally unserviceable condition. Upon this point his testimony certainly cannot be questioned. He shows that a new track has been laid, new engines and cars supplied, and valuable branch roads subsidized to the interests of the main line. All this is likewise true. But will the improvements pointed out account for the missing dividends? Are the scores of suits against the managers of the road for violations of trust or individual rights consistent with the character of a well-managed line? These are among the questions which the report leaves between the Erie President and his shareholders, and upon these points it is not the province of any one outside the corporation to decide. If the report exhibits correctly the present condition of the road, the stockholders have cause to congratulate themselves upon their President and its management. That such may be found to be the case, the public will earnestly, if not confidently, venture to hope.

THE "HOWL AGAINST ERIE"—JUSTICE TO GOULD AND FISK.

From the Paterson Daily Guardian, Jan. 24, 1870.

We ask every reader who desires to form an unprejudiced opinion respecting the Erie Railroad management, to read the highly interesting and instructive Annual Report to the stockholders. It seems to us to be most conclusive, and ought to satisfy all fair-minded men that the Erie Company will in a year or two make it the best paying road in the world. It has monopolized the important branch railroads, has purchased a great stretch of river front, and its terminal, as well as its carrying facilities, can hardly be realized without a careful perusal of the facts in detail, published in our paper to-day.

Let every citizen who has been disposed to lend an ear to the "howl against Erie," read the *facts* as set forth in the report to-day printed, and learn that there is quite a different state of things existing from that attempted to be impressed upon the public mind.

After all, the contest in this State is between the Delaware, Lackawanna and Western Railroad, a heartless and soulless monopoly of faith-breaking propensities (see by the report in to day's paper) and the Erie.

Our people must remember that it was the Erie Railroad which broke down the high price monopoly of coal. We must remember that the Erie Company keeps our shops busy manufacturing locomotives and iron bridges. Why, then, should our people be dragooned into a deadly hostility to the Erie? Our interests demand the Midland R. R. also for Paterson, but we must not forget that to the Erie we owe much of our prosperity as a town and our wealth as a city, and we will always have to rely upon the Erie for the greater portion of our accommodation.

As for Paterson and the Erie, we do not hesitate to say what everybody will admit, that we never had better accomodations for passengers upon the Erie than under the administration of Messrs. Gould & Fisk, and that no town on any other road has such beautiful and commodious cars on its accommodation lines. Let our citizens feel ready and willing to give justice to Messrs. Gould & Fisk in that they have placed the road and its whole equipment in perfect order. When they took hold of it, it was going downward with fearful rapidity. If with their purchase of branch lines and extended improvements they have not been able to create (in addition to all this increased valuation,) heavy dividends, the stockholders may rest assured that the time is not far distant when every stockholder will feel grateful to its present management for establishing it throughout its length and breadth upon such a basis as will make it permanently successful and eminently profitable.

THE BEST ABUSED CORPORATION IN CHRISTENDOM.

A YEAR'S WORK ON THE ERIE RAILWAY.

From the Buffalo Courier, Jan. 25, 1870.

That best abused corporation in this or any other country, the Erie Railway Company to wit, have presented through Jay Gould, President, their eighth annual report, comprising a history in detail of the operations of the road for the fiscal year ending September 30, 1869. "It is something over a year," says Mr. Gould, "since the present management came into power. The condition of the road at that time was not such as to attract the confidence of the traveling public, nor of the shippers of the products of eastern manufactories and of importers to the western states, and of the products of the west to the eastern markets. The iron used in the track had been of an inferior quality, and was much of it worn out and unsafe; this, coupled with the accident at Carr's Rock the previous spring, was injuring the business of the road, both passenger and freight, to such an extent that I felt it my duty to adopt the most effective measures at once."

What has been done, and with what results the action has been accompanied, the report details.

Mr. Gould's first effort was directed to the substitution of steel rails for the worn out iron of the road. There have been laid on the Eastern and Delaware divisions nearly 100 miles of solid steel rails—ten miles of American manufacture and the remainder procured from the best experienced manufacturers of England. Besides these, a large extent of track has been laid with steel headed rail, rolled at the Trenton mills. In all, about four hundred miles of track have been relaid, the present condition of which is said to be "equal if not superior to any in the country, and the reputation of this road in this respect is fully established, as is fully demonstrated by our large and constantly increasing passenger traffic.

The management has decided to adopt iron bridges for all future renewals, and in addition to several small bridges, there has been constructed, during the year, one large iron bridge 650 feet long —four spans—for the crossing of the Susquehanna river.

To renovate the dilapidated locomotive stock of the road, fifty new engines have been purchased and an unlimited amount of repairing done.

* * * * * * * *

[*Here follow long extracts from the Report*] Mr. Gould proceeds to give an account of the Pavonia Ferry and the connecting Horse Railroad to Hudson City, both of which have felt the inspiration of the Erie Management during the year. With regard to the Opera House offices, Mr. Gould gives a brief and plain statement—the building was the only suitable one which could be obtained. Passing from the consideration of the domestic arrangements of the Company, Mr. Gould glances at their " foreign relations.' The problem presented on the incoming of the present management was to break up the combinations of rival trunk lines which threatened to cut off the Erie from all profitable connections.

In concluding his able and impartial criticism of the report the editor says: " IF ANY CORPORATION MANAGEMENT CAN SHOW A BIGGER YEAR'S WORK THAN THIS OF WHICH WE HAVE SKETCHED THE OUTLINES, IT HAS NOT YET BEEN HEARD FROM ! "

THROUGH FROM THE MISSISSIPPI.

From the Waverly Enterprise February 1, 1870.

This magnificent thoroughfare is fully realizing the wildest predictions of its early projectors and builders, under its present splendid management. The gentlemen who now direct its great energies fully comprehend the idea which it incarnates. The main track was settled down upon the earth through a country so geographically conformed and related that if the proper enterprise were combined in its management a vast area of territory North, East, South and West must pour over it an incalculable traffic. The present management, as we have remarked, are wise, broad and sagacious enough to perceive and measure the full magnitnde of their trust, and they have the enterprise and energy to push these views of its destiny to successful demonstration. All interested in the material growth of this State, and particularly of this section, have read the Annual Report of Jay Gould, the President of this road. Its statements of the enterprises accomplished and those inaugurated read almost like romance. Westward they have pushed their enterprise. Other roads running Rocky Mountain-ward—running beyond to the shores of the Pacific—they have bought outright or perpetually subsidized. "Through from the Mississippi." This is the amazing information that procession after procession of freight loaded cars conveys to us who stand here, a thousand miles this side of that mighty river, and gaze at the passing trains sweeping constantly by. North and South after passing through Bergen Hill, the giant begins to throw out its far-reaching arms. Through every mountain gap that leads to a rich land of minerals, or up and down vallies teeming with the still growing wealth of the fields. We shall not attempt in the brief space allotted us, to enumerate the many enterprises of large magnitude this company have prosecuted to results and those being pushed to completion. All of the richest and largest coal and iron fields of northern and middle Pennsylvania they have reached with the shortest and most practicable lines, connecting the great coal traffic with the commerce of the north, the lakes and the great West. Some months since we undertook to show the influence upon the business prospects of this place by the completion of the L. V. R. R , and of the proposed arrangements for conducting the coal traffic. Our vaticinations looked to many then as rather airy. The present facts are fully realizing them. Then President Gould speaks very plainly about the great importance of the Waverly connection and of the future growth of the business here. We have no doubt that there is much ill-blood, outside of any interest in the management of this great railway, at the bottom of the bitter and persistent abuse and persecution which the managing officers encounter. The road is emphatically *our great thoroughfare* of travel and trade. So long as its vast business is shown to increase so rapidly and its great enterprises, such as the opening up of other lines, and the building up of immense trade along the main trunk, are pushed forward to success, we who are directly interested in its success should stand by its officers.

ERIE TO BE THE WEALTHIEST CORPORATION ON THE CONTINENT.

From the Hudson County Daily Democrat, Feb. 5, 1870.

We have read with much satisfaction the Eighth Annual Report of the Erie Railroad. It develops a far-seeing and comprehensive energy, as well as a marvelous industry, on the part of the present managers. Taking hold of its affairs when they were at the lowest ebb, with a depleted treasury, an impaired condition of the railway, a disorganized state of all its resources, and a fairly worn-out equipment, they have, in little more than one year, regenerated and reorganized the road, so as to make it one of the best, if not the very best, on this continent. Traversing, as it does, the richest and most important regions for trade, its magnificent advantages had been hitherto neglected, until, at the touch of the most remarkable genius, its wonderful resources have been developed beyond precedent, considering the difficulties which had to be surmounted. Not only has the main trunkway been repaired and fortified upon a secure foundation, but it has been made to stretch its Briarean arms on every side, seeking out and grasping the incalculable wealth of the most productive regions in the country, and making it tributary to its own success, as well as the general benefit of commerce.

No one can read the clear, business like and truthful report of the President, Mr. Jay Gould, without feeling lost in astonishment at what has been accomplished in so brief a space of time, under such seemingly overpowering embarrassments. The well-considered and comprehensive arrangements which have been made by the present direction, seem to give an assurance of permanent prosperity and usefulness, far beyond the ordinary calculations, even of so great an enterprise. Nothing appears, however, to have been left to speculation, but every estimate is based upon sound business principles. Diversified and vast as the scheme of its new organization is, the plans will bear the closest scrutiny, and the logical results of every proposition, so far as we are capable of comprehending the matter, appear inevitably to vindicate the forecast and wisdom of the management. All along the line of the road connections have been made with a view, not only to economy and profit in the transactions of its own business, but to the more perfect development of the industrial interests of the great productive regions through which it passes, and with which it has established communications. So that whatever may be said by speculators, or rivals of the gentlemen who have wrought this change in the affairs of the "Erie," commerce and industry, from the great West to the Atlantic seaboard, must feel the invigorating influences of their policy, and the people will owe them a debt of gratitude to be measured only by the immense advantages which have been conferred.

Our space will not allow us to review in detail Mr. Gould's report, so as to give facts and figures which he sets forth; but the system which has been adopted is truly wonderful for its comprehensiveness and complexity; but no less so for the order and harmony by which its results are simplified and made to conduce to the benefit of the public, as well as the prosperity of the corporation.

The outlay has unquestionably been large; but the results promise to more than justify the expenditures by the steady and permanent increase of business secured. As an evidence of the success of the system we instance a statement of the receipts of the road under its present management, and those of the previous year. In 1869 the revenue from the passenger traffic shows an increase of over half a million of dollars, while from the freight traffic the increase for the same time is near two millions. This has been accomplished in a single year, and under adverse circumstances; but with the improved facilities of the road a much larger margin may be fairly anticipated.

The property acquired under the present management has been most judiciously selected, and must add largely to its business facilities and to the value of the stock, making it hereafter the wealthiest corporation on the continent, if not in the world.

Now we have nothing to do with what is said of the outside business of Messrs. Gould and Fisk; the Erie road is our objective point, and a most important and interesting subject it is for us Jerseymen, especially in Hudson County, and therefore the conduct of these gentlemen in its affairs becomes a legitimate matter of scrutiny with us, and we say frankly, in the light of a careful observation of their administration that they have displayed an ability and fidelity to their trust which well deserves the gratitude and confidence of the public.

FAIR PLAY FOR THE ERIE.

From the St. Louis Times, January 16, 1870.

A correspondent of the Cincinnati *Enquirer* comes to the rescue of the Erie road against the army of detractors. He is heartily sick, and reasonably so, of the fuss and misrepresentations of the press concerning this road and its management, and thinks it has received anything but "fair play." In support of his convictions, he relates his recent experience, which is daily that of thonsands of others, and from which we extract the following: "I have recently returned to Cincinnati from the East over this line, and all I have to say is, that if the Erie is badly managed, I wish all the roads in the country were badly managed too. It is, without any exception, the most comfortable line I ever traveled over. A great portion of its track has been recently furnished with new rails; and a railroad superintendent, whose ability and judgment has been acquired by thirty years' experience, assured me that he never in his whole life rode over a smoother or safer track than that from New York to Cincinnati by this route. He is not interested in the line, and would hardly have given so warm a commedation unless it were deserved. I certainly never was in coaches more elegant in adornment, substantial in structure or easy in motion, while for safety the fact stands out that in the last year but one passenger, out of 800,000 carried over the Atlantic and Great Western portion of the route, lost his life, and he, confessedly, by his own negligence. On the whole way homeward I watched the advertised time table closely, and have never, in considerable travel, seen one adhered to so closely and certainly. In short, I was never on a better, and I think I never was on so good a line of road before.

MORE GOOD WORDS.

From the Turf, Field and Farm, February 18, 1870.

We heartily concur with the correspondent of the Cincinnati *Enquirer*, and with the St. Louis *Times*, in their commendations of the Erie. We have traveled much upon this road, and as it is the thoroughfare for all the valuable horses traveling to and from the West, to meet their turf engagements, we have had occasion more than once to see Mr. Fisk in reference to their transportation.

Recently we suggested, in view of the very great value of such stock, the building of special racehorse vans, such as are used in England. With that decisive promptness so indicative of administrative power, Mr. Fisk at once acceded to our proposition, and promised to build the vans as soon as drawings could be obtained for the gutdance of his workmen.

ERIE FAR AHEAD OF ITS RIVALS.

From the Saginaw Courier, February 19, 1870.

The report of Mr. Jay Gould, President of that much-abused corporation, the Erie Railway Company, shows that improvements, far ahead of what has been accomplished by many of its rivals, have been made to that important line of communication between the East and the West during the year 1869. The road was in bad condition and low in public estimation when the present management took hold of it, a little over a year ago. [Here follow extracts from the report.] This exhibit is a better illustration of the character of the management of the Erie Directors than the clamors of the various stock-jobbing cliques, and shows that in the direction of the practical affairs of the Company there is efficiency and success. The Erie Railway is fast recovering its old time popularity, and with another year of such improvement it will take the lead among the through lines from East to West.

ERIE AT DUNKIRK.

Special Correspondence of Buffalo Eveniny Express, Nov. 9, 1869.

Speculating as to the prospective prosperity of Dunkirk the correspondent writes: "There is not a town in Western New York that has had its equal in variations of its business prospects, but recent changes in connection with the work done here for the Erie Railway Company have terminated the uncertainty heretofore existing, and its future will be marked by a steady increase of its manufacturing interests and consequent addition to its growth and prosperity. The want, hitherto of a certainty of continued employment has retarded, in a great degree, the growth of Dunkirk, but that drawback is removed by the changes lately made by the Erie Railway Company relating to its extensive machine shops in this town. All the shops and machinery at this point are now leased to an association of wealthy capitalists known as the "Brooks Locomotive Company." At least thirty-five locomotives per year are to be built at these works and a very considerable amount of heavy repairing done. The above, with the large business expected from other railways will make the works the most extensive of the kind in the country, and will undoubtedly eventuate in the addition of blast furnaces and rolling mills, employing in the aggregate, thousands of mechanics and laborers.

"Whatever may be said about Messrs. Gould and Fisk, neglect of the welfare of this road cannot be charged. The road has never had such able executive ability and moved with such perfect regularity as under their direction; and the great increase in its business attests their foresight in preparing for the immeusity of its traffic. But for the superhuman efforts put forth by Messrs. Gould and Fisk, this great Erie Road, with its almost endless ramifications, would have been but an attachment, a feeder to the Central, under the grasping monopoly of Mr. Vanderbilt. If ever the people of the Southern tier of counties and the vast region benefitted by the Erie Railway, had cause to congratulate themselves, it was when the above gentlemen gained permanent control of its management. Nothing that tends to benefit the road escapes their attention, and no undertaking too immense to prevent its accomplishment if desired for the welfare of the Erie Railway.

"FAIR PLAY IS A JEWEL"

The following is one of the many calls for fair play which have been made from time to time:

NEW YORK, SEPTEMBER 18, 1869.

Editors New York Express.

Will you permit a constant reader of your paper, and consequently one desirous of now and then having his "say" regarding current matters, to inquire why it is that the press, not only in this city, but throughout the country, lose no opportunity of dwelling editorily upon every accident occurring along the line of the Erie Railway as an "Erie horror," while they content themselves with a brief mention of any casualties that may happen on any other line? The question occurred to me this morning. Taking up the paper, I read: "Collision on the Central Railroad—an entire passenger train disabled." Ah, thought I, we shall have another homily from the editor on the subject of railway mismanagement. But, to my surprise, there was no comments to be seen elsewhere; nor had any of the other papers, as I afterwards found, a word more than the simple recital of the fact.

Now, Mr. Editor, I don't care a fig for one railway more than another. They may, as far as I am personally concerned, go as fast as the winged steed Pegasus, or as slow as Sisyphus, laboring at his up-hill task. I rarely ride, and own no shares; you may, therefore, rely on my discriminations when I say that the Erie, which, to my observation, advertises more liberally than any other line, is by the general press most unfairly and illiberally treated. Let us have a variety of horrors—a "Central horror," a "Pan-handle horror," or else give us no horror at all.

A VETERAN OBSERVER.

FISK A SHREWD MANAGER AND ORGANIZER.

From the Evening Telegram, Nov. 27, 1869.

That bright little sheet, the *Evening Telegram*, which frequently serves as pilot fish to the *Herald* and its "blanket sheet" contemporaries, shows its superior penetration in the following article:

THE ERIE-PRESSIBLE CONFLICT.—The schemers and plotters engaged in the buying, selling and holding of railway stocks are determined to keep themselves everlastingly before the public, and the most important and notorious line to operate on being the Erie Railway—they generally select this road for the purpose of creating excitement. The Erie Railway has been highly unfortunate for the past twenty years. The broad and narrow guage war waged at Erie some eighteen or nineteen years ago was the inauguration of the strife, then the unhappy selection of a $25,000 President and an imbicile board of directors, soon drove the road into the hands of a receiver. It was not until the redoubtable Fisk, Jr., obtained control, that this road has been in a semi-decent condition. With all of Fisk's faults, the fact of his being a shrewd manager and organizer cannot be denied. His great ambition to unite the Erie Railway with every road leading West is not only practical and important, but this very importance raises the ire of his enemies, hence the injunctions and counter injunctions which are issued almost daily. These legal squabbles, if carried on much longer, will in themselves become criminal, as the only result is the robbing of the stockholders of their interests and fattening up of the hungry droves of lawyers.

A GROWING SENSE OF JUSTICE.

American Standard, March 8, 1870.

The attentive observer of current events cannot have failed to perceive of late a very marked change in public opinion in favor of the great Erie Railway, as an avenue of transit to and from the Metropolis, and a very general acknowledgment on the part of the press and the traveling public that the slanders at one time so widely circulated by interested parties, to the prejudice of the line, are not only unfounded in fact but calculated seriously to inconvenience travelers, by inducing them to take more circuitous and less luxurious modes of journeying. The truth is, the public, never, as a body, far from right in its conclusions, has come to look with mistrust upon the oft-repeated assertions prejudicial to this great route. They find that, notwithstanding all said to the contrary, there is no line which, in point of comfort, punctuality, and reliability, offers such inducements as the broad gauge Erie Railway, which delivers its westward-bound passengers either at Buffalo, Dunkirk, Cleveland or Cincinnati, without change of cars, and provides for their comfort and accommodation, during the journey, spacious and luxurious coaches, provided with all the accessories of a first-class hotel parlor or bed-room, and fitted up in a style which can only be compared to the fabled glories of the palace of Sardanapalus. Seeing and appreciating all this, the American traveler unconsciously exclaims, "Can this be the road which has been so persistly represented as unsafe, irregular, and inconvenient to travelers? If so, [to use the words of a recent correspondent of the Cincinnati Enquirer], all I have to say is, I wish all the roads in the country were "badly managed, too. It is, without exception, the most comfortable line I ever traveled over." And this testimony is daily corroborated by scores of people, who, prompted by curiosity or by the advice of those who have already traveled over the line, give Erie the preference, and before their journey is half over, are enthusiastic in their admiration of its merits. Every day this reaction is more apparent in the augmented demand at all the central offices for through tickets, in the increased length of the passenger trains leaving Jersey City every morning and evening, and in the construction of some elegant new Sleeping Coaches, which for beauty and luxury of finish must be seen to be appreciated. Public opinion, long misled by the industriously circulated slanders of rivals, is at last becoming settled in the conviction that there is but one great National route between the West and East, and that is the Broad Gauge Erie Railway.

A FRIENDLY WORD FOR FISK AND GOULD.

From the Scranton, Pa., Daily Democrat, January 25, 1870.

These two great railroad magnates seem to be the object of the spite and envy of a great many people now-a-days; especially do we find the radical press pitching into them without gloves. Now, we have never seen anything of either of these gentlemen that should occasion the pouring out of such vials of wrath upon their devoted heads, as every once in a while comes spat upon our eyes and ears. What it all means is rather a mystery to us, especially that our neighbor across the way should take so much pains to traduce them. Men of such remarkable ability and whose career exhibits such wonderful success, will always have their villifiers; but when we see them traveling away out of their ordinary course to bespatter their slime, it looks as though there might be a "nigger in the fence." The duce of it is with us, is to know just where that nigger is, and what he is there for.

Certainly the management of the New York and Erie has never been so able, as under the manipulations of these gentlemen. If they have been looking out for themselves, about which we neither know nor care, they have kept steadily in view the prosperity of their great road, until now, associated with its connecting links, it almost spans the continent. Under their control, too, they have brought the New York and Erie into our valley, a circumstance in connection with our prosperity and future welfare we can hardly at this time appreciate. It does seem to us that men of such enlarged and liberal views should rather be the recipients of the good wishes of our people than their kicks, and if they have been a little too much for the infernal rascals with whom they have been thrown in association so much the better.

Hurrah for Fisk and Gould. More anon.

HOW THE ROAD IS WORKED.

From the New York Democrat, December 9, 1869.

The Erie trains go and come on the Erie with marvelous promptness, notwithstanding the great snow storm. The track is kept clear, and the trains come in on time, full laden with passengers from the West, who give the Erie preference over all other roads. The Division Superintendents and track-masters on that road, with all others connected with the running of trains, take great pride in doing well the work confided to their care, and by so doing make this one of the most popular roads in the country for travel. No matter how Erie stock is quoted, the *Erie Railway* is always above par.

VANDERBILT AND ERIE.

From the New York Evening Commonwealth, November 22, 1869.

The public have often been obliged to disapprove of certain doings of " the Erie people," as Messrs. Fisk and Gould are popularly called. There is one movement, however, that these gentlemen are making in which they will have the best wishes of a large majority of the public. Commodore Vanderbilt last year tried to get possession of the Erie Railroad, as he had already done of the Hudson River and the New York Central. Had he succeeded, he would have become the monopolist of every avenue from the West to this port. All traffic would have had to pay toll to him, and that healthful competition which is so essential to the public good, would have been at an end. Mr. Vanderbilt, conscious of his financial strength, set to work to buy up all the stock that he could get, and spent several millions of dollars in this effort. The Erie Company, claiming that they had legal power, issued a large amount of new stock. The Commodore, finding that his purse was not long enough to buy the new stock as well as the old, gave up the attempt, and several suits were at once brought against the Erie

Company, and the disgraceful scandals of this litigation are fresh in the memories of our readers. *It is remarkable, however, that although Commodore Vanderbilt's name was not seen in any of these suits, still the Company paid four millions of dollars to him, and the suits were all compromised or withdrawn.*

Now, all this was done by the *old* Board of Directors of the Erie road. The *present* Board repudiate the bargain, and bring a suit to recover back the Company's money. The Commodore was in court on Saturday, and his testimony amounts substantially to this—that he sold at 80, fifty thousand shares of the Erie stock he bought last year; that his stock was sold to Daniel Drew, and not the Erie Railway Company, and that he engaged to sell 50,000 shares more at the same price, if required to do so, within twelve months; that in consideration of these stipulations, he received $3,500,000 in cash, and $500,000 worth of bonds of the Boston, Hartford and Erie Company. The whole case turns on two points: first, whether the transaction is one which the Erie Board were legally competent to perform; and, secondly, whether if competent, the Erie Company did actually complete the negotiation, or, whether *it was done by Daniel Drew in his personal, individual character.*

THE LAST ERIE STRIKE.

Experience has demonstrated that strikes are seldom, if ever, productive of any good result, either to labor or capital. The last Erie strike would appear to be an exception however—the benefit being with the Company. The loss of the Jersey City malcontents is considered a gain, not only by their late employers, but by the better class of their fellow craftsmen all along the line. It is asserted that they were always trying to create some difficulty, and that in discharging themselves in a body they have saved the trouble of weeding them out one by one. No difficulty was experienced in filling their places with men fully equal in mechanical skill and vastly superior in all other respects. The total failure of this last strike is considered a great triumph for the Company, and the opinion prevails among the employes of the road that it will be the last for some time to come. Under the loose administration of the old management, the men in all the departments did pretty much as they pleased, and striking became a chronic disorder. *Mais, nous avons changez tout cela.* Since the present dynasty ascended the throne of Erie, the different departments have been thoroughly overhauled and reformation has been the order of the day. Among the first to feel the power of the new regime were the corrupt conductors, and no better evidence of their guilt is needed than the enormous increase in the passenger returns which followed their summary discharge. Figures do not lie, and the books of the Company prove that these men were as arrant a set of knaves as ever "took to the road." Next came the old brakemen, who, flushed with a dozen victories over the effete administration, which preceded the present, sought once more to assert their supremacy over their employers and extort increased pay. But in Gould and Fisk they found they had men of far different metal to deal with and consequently they failed ignominously and made way for better men. Last came the Jersey City mechanics; and their recent fiasco, however disastrous to themselves, cannot fail to be productive of much good to their more sensible fellow craftsmen at the different shops along the line. All that was necessary to enforce proper discipline in the ranks of Erie was pluck and determination—attributes with which the present management is abundantly well endowed and which their predecessors lacked utterly.

LABOR VERSUS CAPITAL.

The Erie managers and the employes of the road are equally indebted to the *Commercial Advertiser* for the following sensible article on the little difficulties which occasionally arise between them:

"Whatever may be thought of the Erie Railway management, one thing is very certain, the public do not look with favor upon the demonstrations made by the employes of the road. Affairs have reached a high pass if laborers can, with impunity, demand of capitalists the removal of this and that overseer or manager, and the restoration of this or that employe. Once let such demands be complied with and all the natural relations existing between labor and capital will be disarranged. If men choose to foolishly strike for higher wages they have a perfect right to do so. But they have no right to attempt to bully, intimidate, or force their employers to accede to any or every request which they may see fit to make. Because the Erie employes were partially successful in their late demonstration they make bold to begin another. Let these new demands be acceded to and why will they not in a short time make still others? What is to prevent railroad employes all over the country from organizing against their respective corporations, and under the threat of stopping travel, force compliance with arbitrary and unjust demands?

For our part we approve of the past course pursued by the Erie managers in this matter. They have done exactly right in saying to these disaffected employes we will not yield a whit more to your demands, but will, if need be, resort to compulsory efforts for cleaning you out and filling your places with new men. This matter of labor revolt against capital is being carried altogether too far, under the impetus resulting from the success which has attended strikes in various branches of employment. It is high time for the press to bring its influence to bear upon such organized disorganization, before capital is paralysed all over the country. As for railroad malcontents, they are pursuing just the course to lead railroad corporations to combine against them, and establish uniform rates, ruling considerably lower than those now paid. Our advice to them is, to hold up in their career of folly at once, if they would avert such a combination. There are tens of thousands of men wanting employment all over the State, and the labors connected with railroading are by no means so difficult that new hands cannot very soon acquire "the handling of the ropes."

THE LAST ERIE STRIKE.

The New York *Evening Express* of Jan, 26, gives the following editorial opinion of the last Erie strike: "The men in the Erie workshops discharged themselves, and like the dog in the manger, would neither work themselves nor permit others to work. They had a perfect right to quit work if they chose, but their attempt to coerce other laborers, as well as their late employers, was wholly without excuse."

REPORT OF THE HERALD COMMISSIONER.

So many conflicting reports being in circulation as to the condition of the Erie road, and the conduct of its vast business, and to the necessity of an impartial investigation in the interest of the travelling public, and of those who had invested their money in the securities of the corporation being so obvious, the *Herald*, with the liberality and enterprise which is its distinguishing characteristic under the present young and vigorous management sent a special commissioner to make a thorough survey of the line. The following extracts from the Report of the *Herald* Commissioner need no further introduction and but little in the way of comment.

Writing from Port Jervis, under the date Jan. 17, 1870, the correspondent gives the opinions of the workmen at that point on the foolish conduct of the Jersey city malcontents, who, it will be remembered, only succeeded in "striking" their names off the company's pay-roll, and supplies much valuable evidence showing the utter falsity of the oft-repeated assertions that the present management was "extremely unpopular," &c., &c.

"Do the employes regard the present management as unreliable and unsatisfactory?" asked the representative of the *Herald* of a representative mechanic.

"No," he responded. "On the contrary, *the road was never managed better*, and I myself look upon the complaints made by certain people, as just what folks will say when they are knocked out of easy, profitable positions. I recollect a time *when everybody on this road appeared to do as he d—d pleased, but now things are changed*, and fellows have got to show something for the money that's paid them."

The Port Jervis letter concludes as follows: "The most satisfactory thing, however, to discover here is that all the trains run on time, and that there is no falling of in freight or passengers."

From the New York Herald, Jan. 21, 1870.

THE FEELING ALONG THE ROAD.

THE TROUBLES AND ITS CAUSES—ABSENCE OF SYMPATHY AND EXPRESSIONS OF CENSURE—ALL ABOUT THE ROAD AND ITS MANAGEMENT.

SUSQUEHANNA, Pa., Jan. 18, 1870.

There is no strike here and no likelihood of any occurring. Those reports to the effect that the men here and at Port Jervis sympathized with their fellow craftsmen in Jersey City in the present difficulty and expressed their determination to join them I find are altogether unfounded. From this standpoint the strike is looked upon as a rash, inconsiderate and altogether unwise movement, productive of no good, injurious to the interests of the men themselves and decidedly incapable of securing any greater harmony in the future between the company and its workmen.

As it was stated in the letter from Fort Jervis, the men there discountenanced the action of their brethren in Jersey City, because of its ill-timed character, but here I find they not only view it in the same light, but they consider there has been a most unwarranted trifling with the legitimate purpose of the association. They say an agreement was entered into that when a positive grievance to their interests was inflicted by the company a strike should be simultaneously entered upon, but no difficulty of the kind that happened at Jersey City, and which might have been quietly and quickly adjusted, afforded sufficient grounds for a number of men quitting their customary work and involving themselves and their families in embarrassment. When such sentiments are held by those who of all others should be most in sympathy with the strikers, there must be something radically wrong in the whole affair, and attention is naturally directed to the nature of the employments which the men follow, their pay, their prospects and the capacity of the road to which they belong. The outside public are apt to suppose, when hearing of a railroad strike, that everybody attached to the concern has put on his hat and left. The brakeman has given a last disgusted turn to the wheel, the conductor made a final and fretful punch in a passenger's ticket, the engineer jumped from his sad and silent locomotive, the switchman made a pocket handkerchief of his signal flag, and all the rest of the railroad army have shaken the dust from their feet and struck out' for a change of air. The idea is, of course a delusion

This road, with a much exaggerated strike at one end of it, is working just the same as if no commotion whatever had occurred; and even if all the shops here and elsewhere were empty of their industrious inmates, the road, it seems to me, could get along for a considerable time without them. It is an old and extensive road, with an enormous supply on hand of all that material which forms the product of the mechanic's labor. It has more locomotives than it can conveniently use, and as for cars they are reckoned by thousands. To building and repairing locomotives the labor of the machinists is directed, and they are the men who almost entirely monopolize the glorious privilege of striking. The car builders do not share in the luxury, as they hold themselves aloof from the organization. The brakemen once struck, but it broke them down from a sheer miscalculation of their mechanical value. They were swept out on the instant and twice as many other brakemen offered their services next morning. The strike of the machinists interferes with nothing in the line of travel, whether of freight or passenger trains. All these run just as usual, and the general work of the road is in no wise disturbed.

EFFECT OF THE STRIKE ON THE COMPANY.

It is dobutful if a body of mechanics could select a more unimpressionable corporation to operate upon at this particular time than the Erie. Their supply of rolling stock is so large that they have been forced to reduce the working capacity of the shops, and mechanical labor is consequently at a discount. Again, judging from the character of public opinion here, the new management, embracing the blonde and bold Prince of Erie—the immortal Jim Fisk, Jr.—and Prime Minister Jay Gould, are credited with a share of determination that promises to put an end to strikes forever. They will stamp out disaffection or perish in the attempt, while at the same time they show every disposition to agree to anything reasonable. Fisk has a curious reputation up this way. People think he stumbled on the lamp of Aladdin, and some fine day will come up to Susquehanna and turn its barren hills into virgin gold. Gould is very popular with the railroad men. They say he knows a locomotive from the nose of the cowcatcher to the coupling at her tail end, can run with the machine, plan a bridge, lay a rail, switch a freight train and divers other things too numerous to mention. The truth is, one has to leave home to learn the news. We gave Gould credit enough for raising "old Harry" in Wall street, but it is hardly within the popular estimate of his abillity that he could drive a locomotive and keep out of a smashup. Candidly speaking and after impartial investigation, the present management, whoever they are, have done vastly for this road, which anybody who knew it some years ago will readily admit. In the work of improvement and reformation they have to contend with established prejudices with old, venerable employes, of comparatively stage coach notions and with lazy and turbulent labor.

To get a proper appreciation of what is disturbed in the workings of the Erie Railroad by a strike of machinists, it is necessary to give some idea of the class of men employed, the interests involved, the kind of work done and the scale upon which it is performed. A sketch of the shops at this point will, therefore, be appropriate, while at the same time the views here and there of some of the men will tend to shed a better light upon the subject.

VIEWS OF ONE OF THE MEN.

Mr. T. J. Mayo, engine despatcher, in answer to the question as to the cause of the strike in Jersey City, replied:—"I believe if the association makes a demand of men all along the road to strike for the purpose of supporting those in Jersey City there will be a split in the camp here and very few will respond to the summons. You see, most of the mechanics with us who have been here any time possess property in real estate, and perhaps design spending all their lives in Susquehanna. The whole population, of course, depends upon the road and take an interest in it. In 1848, when the company concluded to select this place for a leading point on the line, they bought 300 acres of land, and after putting up their shops upon it they concluded to dispose of what remained to the employes at a low price. The men saved their earnings, bought lots and put up houses, and naturally feel a concern for the welfare of the town. That large number of houses you may observe scattered over the face of the hill above are owned by men who work in the shops. They are more comfortably situated than any class of mechanics in America, and perhaps more independent. Now these men know the folly of such a strike as the present one and they wont go into it, nor will the men at Port Jervis; but those at Jersey City and Buffalo are a different class. They are unsettled and floating, without much to lose from a strike and ready for one at any time."

"Is there any cause of complaint here?" I inquired.

"None that I know of," replied Mr. Mayo. "We were promptly paid, and I can't see any reason for trouble. I have been connected with the road a good many years, and I don't know that it was ever better managed than it is now. Within the last two years there has been a big change for the better, and if the same management continues a little while longer there won't be any fault to find with Erie. We have fresh, new locomotives, freight and passenger cars added to the rolling stock every day; new road bed for miles, steel rails, iron culverts, new bridges built of iron going up in place of the old wooden ones, and a hundred other improvements that go to make a railroad complete according to the English standard. These strikes don't agree with our people here, because they want to see the road go ahead, and such things have a bad effect, but I think this is the last of them you will see for some time. The management will hardly stand it any longer."

Other men like Mr. Mayo spoke in a similar way, indicating more censure than sympathy for the movement in Jersey City. There is no question that officials have it frequently in their power to annoy and harrass those immediately under them, and that the exercise of such authority may lead to a strike without the Company being directly responsible.

HOW SUSQUEHANNA WOULD SUFFER.

Some idea of the disastrous results which would happen to the natives of Susquehanna from a strike may be formed from the fact that the Erie Company disburse for wages at this point from $30,000 to $35,000 per month. A strike enduring for a term of two weeks would consequently involve a loss of at least $15,000. But this fails to a measure the extent of pecuniary embarrassment entailed; for it is easy to see that a large body of men idle for two weeks will encroach upon their savings considerably, and, perhaps, dissipate all they laid by. Then there are many other ways in which the thing works injuriously. It breeds ill feeling and leaves irritation after it; for whichever side loses is bound to take the first opportunity for revenge.

A RAILROAD RIDE.

An invitation from Mr. J. T. Camero, to the new experience of taking an airing in the fresh and early morning, was accepted by your correspondent, and under the guidance of Messrs. Mayo and Atwater we started a mile or so down the road from here to see one of the great wonders of American engineering, the Starrucca viaduct.

This immense structure is so like the High Bridge that the visitor from New York fancies himself on the banks of Spuyten Duyvil creek. It is 1,200 feet in length, 110 feet in height, and has eighteen arches. Looking up at it from below, at its vast and solid buttresses, one is tempted to believe for a moment that this work of man's hands will last as long as the eternal hills upon which its extremities repose. Having satisfied our curiosity well and fully we again mounted our steam carriage and flew away past Susquehanna a short distance to see another bridge—one of iron— in process of being built.

The original structure was of wood, but here was the iron going in, rod and bolt and bar replacing the beams of wood and lifting up a light, airy and strong framework of metal many hundreds of feet long over the turbid and brawling Susquehanna. We stayed a brief time; talked with the accomplished engineer, Mr. S. S. Post, and then rattled back to view the celebrated

ENGINEER'S QUARTERS OF THE SUSQUEHANNA WORKS.

They are very complete indeed—neat, clean and handsome as the drawing room of the best hotel—a place for everything and everything in its proper place. The building is devoted exclusively to the use of the men who drive the locomotives, and has done a world of good in bringing them together in a pleasant, sociable way, and with the attractions of a sitting and reading room, where books and papers furnish a relaxation from the fatiguing labors of the day. This is a great trout fishing region, and in one of the lower rooms of the engineers' quarters a big tub, like a tank, contains a countless shoal of minnows to serve as bait when they go on their piscatorial rambles up the higher waters of the lovely Susquehanna.

A GLIMPSE AT THE WORKSHOPS.

But it is the workshops proper that give a character and an importance to this place. They cover over six acres and employ altogether something like a thousand men. They are under the management of a gentleman named Mr. J. B. Gregg, who has been over twenty-five years connected with the road. The machine shop is 774 feet long by 138 wide. Its interior appearance, when all the slippery belts are moving to and fro overhead in a seemingly endless series and the machinery beneath is polishing, pairing, punching and hammering the thousand things that make up the anatomy of a locomotive, has an extremely impressive appearance. Here the steam-engine, so familiar to the eyes of the million, with its funnel-shaped smokestack and polished belts of brass, is built from the foundation up. There you see them as you look along in all stages of construction and in all stages of repair. They stand in a long, imposing row, like soldiers on parade, and look as if they could carry the house away with them if the steam was turned on. Nothing strikes the visitor so much as the scrupulous cleanliness and order of this immense workshop. You fancy for a moment you are in some great government arsenal, and the impression is confirmed in looking at the determined, clear cut military features of your chaperone, Mr. Gregg. His face is in fact one of methodistic severity. Not a scrap of iron lies loose around, and you walk between the huge locomotives lifted off their legs several feet above their ordinary level without having occasion to step an inch aside by reason of any rubbish lying in your path. All along one side of the building benches are ranged of curiously complicated machinery, which performs the nice fine work of turning out finished pieces of brass and steel that one notices stuck here and there around a locomotive. Not many men seem to be attending these machines, for they are of such improved and semi-automatic character that they need but a limited guidance from human hands.

No better idea of the magnitude of the railroad and its traffic can be had than in looking through this shop at its colossal collections of machinery and the capacity it exhibits to perform an immense measure of labor. Adjoining the machine department are the boiler shop, 200 feet by 116; blacksmith shop, 180 by 86; carpenter shop, 120 by 70; pattern shop, 120 by 70; paint shop, 120 by 60; pattern storeroom, 120 by 60; coppersmith, tin, and sheet-iron shop, 120 by 50; storeroom, 120 by 50; foundry, 200 by 62; cleaning room, 85 by 40; sand room, 100 by 25;

engine room for foundry, 35 by 20; engine room for shops, 85 by 25; and the hammer shop, which contains several steam hammers, the heaviest being a 2,200 pounder. The semi-circular engine house near at hand has accomodation for forty locomotives, the most of that number being generally under its shelter in reserve.

OTHER WORKS OF THE COMPANY.

A gas manufactory belonging to the company supplies the works with light. Adjoining the machine. shop is the superintendent's office, and in the same building are a well-appointed library and reading-room for the men, and a lecture hall that need fear no disparaging comparison with any outside of Philadelphia. The different departments are heated by about 200 miles of steam pipes. A Corliss engine of 100 horse power drives the machinery of the shops, and a fire engine of 100 pounds pressure is ever ready to throw a powerful stream of water on any conflagration that may occur. All the buildings are built of massive stone and substantial brick work, and, taken altogether, with the order and cleanliness everywhere apparent, form, perhaps, the most complete railroad workshops in the country. About a stone's throw from the works the company have a hotel, known as the Starrucca House, which in its appointments beats anything of the kind known this side of New York. The dining room is like a baronial banqueting hall, or the transcept section of a Gothic Cathedral. It is 120 feet by 40, and 50 feet from the floor to the roof. The whole of Susquehanna might be comfortably fed within its capacious and gorgeous interior, and it is no unmerited eulogy to say that its meals are of a higher order than those of Mugby Junction.

From the New York Herald, January 29th.

THE ERIE MANAGEMENT.

THE WORKS OF THE ERIE RAILROAD AT ELMIRA—A LIGHT UPON THE ROAD—A CHAPTER OF THE IRON AGE—NATURE OF THE STRIKE AND ITS CONSEQUENCES.

ELMIRA, Jan. 24, 1870.

The further one gets from Jersey City the less interest appears to be taken in the strike which is agitating the souls of the sons of labor at that point. Here the mechanics talk of the subject in as feeble and indifferent a spirit as if it were no concern of theirs whatever. This is easily explained. The men on strike at Jersey City are of a different type of mechanics in this respect, their social surroundings produce an influence on their way of living. and thinking, which has much to do with their ready disposition to start a strike. The men at Jersey City spend more of their earnings, are less tractable and feel less dependent for work on the Erie Company than those at any of the shops intervening between there and Buffalo. At Port Jervis there are restraining influences which have more or less effect on the minds of the workmen, the absence of surrounding attractions in the shape of similar labor outside, in which they might get employment in case of losing what they have; the fact of having a house, and perhaps a lot, and of having a family; and, it may be, an ambition to start some day in the little town in some sort of business. In Jersey City, on the contrary, the mechanic lives after a different and less satisfactory fashion.

MANNER OF LIFE.

His evening resort may be other than his home, his companions are, perhaps, nomadic mechanics, who, having nothing to bind them to one place, are prepared for a strike, and ready to bundle up their traps at a moment's notice and start for other fields and pastures new. At Susquehanna, most of the men have houses and lots of their own; they feel themselves part and parcel of the place, take an interest in its growth and prosperity, live decent, frugal, happy lives, and show no precipitate humor to plunge into a strike without full and due provocation. Here it is a good deal the same way. Living is cheap, the town is quiet, comfortable, and progressing, houses and lots can be bought at a figure within the reach of a prudent and saving mechanic, and therefore it is that the men who know the non-paying character of most strikes, prefer to suffer some inconvenience rather than run the risk of being indefinitely out of employment. At Buffalo, I am told, there is much similar class of mechanics to that of Jersey City—men who have little at stake beyond the loss of a few weeks' wages, and who are generally able by moving off to another point to procure the like kind of work to that which they have left.

AN INFLUENCE OF THE STRIKE.

In talking with Mr. Rathbone, Superintendent of the rolling mills here, he said much of the influence which helped to produce the present strike was due to the efforts of the people, as he called them, of the Rogers Locomotive Works at Paterson, and Paterson folks generally. The feud existing between the Erie Company and the proprietors of the Rogers Works is one of uncommon bitterness. The former once gave an order for thirty engines to a firm in Pennsylvania, and the latter resented the slight by sending their locomotives, manufactured for Western roads, around by Harlem and the New York Central, rather than over the Erie road, which passed by the door, and was a much more and less expensive route. Then the people of Paterson had many of their pleasant traveling privileges abrogated recently, and Erie has, in consequence, come in for some high and healthy criticism. The people of the Rogers works, it is alleged, have tampered with the workmen at Jersey City and supplied the means of carrying on the strike, and it is broadly given out that corporations of a rival character to Erie, and with no sympathy for its fortunes, have secretly fomented the disturbance and kept it alive. Again, it is insinuated that those who profess to lead the disaffected workmen do so to make capital out of it and have no particular wish to hasten an amicable settlement.

From those who are not in sympathy with the strikers the statement is oftentimes made that a class of men have been at work in Jersey City whom it would be good policy for the road to get rid of. They have always been a disturbing element of the workshops and are of no particular ability as mechanics. However it is, one cannot help thinking that many of these strikers are based upon an erroneous and ignorant appreciation of the rights of labor as opposed to capital. The Erie Company had as perfect a right to dismiss their men, even though the number exceeded two or three hundred, as any store on Broadway has to dispense with the services of its clerks —a thing which is frequently done in the dull season. But that the men working away quietly and well in all the other shops, without any cause for complaint, should be called upon to turn out and support the indiscretion of the rest, appears very absurd to sensible men. It is clear that those who seek this method of rectifying their wrongs presume upon the measure of annoyance which they are capable of giving and on the weakness with which they are met. It can hardly be said that this is a right and moral justification of their proceeding, or what is calculated to secure them any real sympathy from the public.

THE SENTIMENT AT ELMIRA.

The mechanics here are a peaceable and industrious set of men, and I understand disconnected with the association called the "Mutual Protective Association of Erie Employes." Asking the superintendent of the car shop if he heard any intention of his men being about to strike, he replied "Not until I tell them." He, however, may be exceptionably situated; for his kindness of manner would smooth over many a difficulty which others less enviable endowed might render a serious and painful embarrassment. As in my letter from Susquehanna, I sought to give some idea of the vast scale on which the mechanical labor of the Erie Railroad is conducted. I will endeavor here to give a sketch of another branch of work equally interesting—the manufacture of cars, freight, passenger, sleeping, and all sorts, together with the immense rolling mill where the rails for the track are turned out at the rate of 2,000 tons a month. As the strike is attracting so much attention the working of the road and the kind of labor at which its mechanics are engaged seems an appropriate subject for description.

THE WORKSHOPS AT ELMIRA.

Opposite and away to the northeast of the Elmira depot are the various shops, apparently scattered in confusion over several acres of land. On coming to make a tour of them you discover there are great method and order in their arrangement, and when you meet Mr. Rutter, the superintendent of the car shops, you find that all of it is due to him—to his tireless industry and love of regularity. As the locomotive at the Susquehanna works rises gradually from a horizontal frame work of iron so does the passenger car lift itself from a curious looking floor of wood braced up and down and every way into a bright and airy structure of light yellow walls, crystal windows and gorgeously decorated interior. Machinery plays an important part in the building of passenger cars. It enters into every feature of construction save the upholstering and painting. People have noticed as they jogged along in an American railroad car of the latest model what a profusion of delicate and artistic work is expended upon the interior. Some folks are apt to think it is a positive extravagance to fit a vehicle up on so lavish a scale of unappreciated decoration. The perfection of the machinery in the car shop explains how easily and cheaply all this thing is done. The old art of carving was a mighty slow and wavering process of fashioning shapes of beauty out of wood. By machinery the work is done in an incredibly brief space of time. On a small table uncomely pieces of walnut are transformed in an instant through the medium of a little piece of steel—worked, of course, by steam—into figures of ornament that the poor wood carver might sigh for a lifetime to imitate in perection of finish. The ease and rapidity with which this is performed are astonishing. The walnut, rosewood, mahogany and other woods that enter into the ornamental part of a first class passenger car are turned out in less time than it takes to write about it.

When the ground floor of the car is completed, resting upon span new iron trucks, it is shoved out of the first car shop into the second, where the sides are built up and the painting done. Improvements have been made from time to time in the general construction; but now it appears a new school of railroad men has sprung up, crying out for light built passenger cars and rolling stock in general as being much superior in point of speed, cheapness, aud comfort, and much better adapted to the railroad of the future. Mr. Rutter, after twenty-one years' experience in building cars, and an enthusiast of the light weights, contrives to take half a ton of wood less than the quantity used for passenger cars some few years ago. This is done in a great variety of ways—by rendering parts hollow, which were hitherto deemed necessary to be put in solid, by introducing thin iron bands where beams were formerly used, and by substituting glue and canvas where boards an inch thick were considered indispensable. A bright, glittering first-class passenger-car, fresh from the hands of the painter, stands on the track outside the shop, and its detailed description is thus given: forty-nine feet long, ten and a half wide; height, in centre, ten and a half, on side, seven feet eight inches, a dome roof running the whole length of the car, thirty seats for sixty passengers, four trucks weighing six and three quarter tons, body of car ten and a quarter tons, four journal and six bolster springs to each axle. Exterior, the standard color yellow; interior finish consisting of walnut panellings between the windows, ornamented with carved sprigs, a fanciful carved piece over each door, and all relieved and set off with gilt mouldings and a panelling in each end—cost of the whole $5,000. Our chaperon tells us of the wonders the shop has performed, the freight cars by the mile it has turned out and repaired, the passenger cars, the hand cars, the caboose cars, and then with a glowing pride he talks of the drawing-room coaches, with their flashing mirrors, Turkey carpets, crimson velvet seats, walnut mouldings, private rooms, and general fittings, grander far than ever a prince before the age of steam could command in riding to his coronation. The painter's studio, the upholster's room, and the polisher's department, are all worth a visit, as showing the variety and completeness of the details necessary to build and fully equip those passenger cars with which people are familiar.

LUXURY ON WHEELS.

But the drawing-room coach, as it stood with all its fittings in, and its light airy frescoing still damp with the paint of the artist, gave the highest notion of the perfection to which this branch of railroad art has been brought. Imagine a whole series of the most richly furnished and elaborately decorated ladies' boudoirs placed side by side and opposite to each other, and some notion may be had of the drawing-room coach. Passing along the thickly-carpeted aisle, the eye glances from left to right with a curious delight in peeping at each new and splendid compartment, and trying to distinguish which is the grandest and most complete. The heavy padding of the crimson plush and the thick folds of the parted curtains made of ruby silk, give a richness of appearance to each cosy compartment of a truly royal character. Then, for lace curtains, you have the large windows embossed around the border in imitation of chantilly, the pattern peeping out from the glass from the folds of the looped up terry. For paintings you have the roof and panels frescoed in a style of art seldom seen outside the canvas of a first-rate picture. At the side are pipes for heating the compartments with hot water, and last of all is the crowning triumph, a gas apparatus for supplying light. In the wide parlor or reception-room lounges, and heavy chairs of red velvet and carpeted cushions for the feet are strewn around. The interior finish is solid walnut, inlaid and veneered with ash buhl, French walnut buhl, and Hungarian ash. The cornices, even, of the door posts attract attention, but the eye, above all, delights to wander over the field of fresco on the wide ceiling. Here the artist seemed to revel iu luxuriance of fancy and variety and brilliancy of color. But a truce to description, for any that can be given would fail to convey fully the luxury and beauty of these drawing-room coaches.

THE RAILROAD ARTISTS.

It is interesting to take a peep at the artist's studio where the designs for car panels are painted. Around the walls are square pieces of canvas slowly drying. One piece contains two different bits of landscape at either side and in the middle; at the top, a Chinese dragon, flourishing his lively tail high in air. This is intended to stretch across one end of the car above the entrance; but the stretch of the canvas is nothing to the stretch of the artist's imagination. All around are sporting, marine and rural pictures on wooden-panels, waiting to be used.

In the upholsterer's room you are let into the secret of how these smooth and handsome velvet seats are made. Great improvements have been introduced in this direction. Light spiral springs, beneath a thin board, now occupy the place of solid wood, and the apparently heavy back feels little heavier than a cigar box. Horse hair is extensively used, but the introduction of springs in the seat backs is the feature of chief interest. The work done by the mechanics is in no instance of a heavy or laborious character. Machinery takes upon itself all that is cumbrous and fatiguing, and only the lighter details need manipulation at the hands of the workmen.

THE TRADES AND WAGES OF THE MEN.

The following are the trades of the men employed and the average rate of wages, working at eight hours per day, the recently reduced term of time:—One superintendent car repairs, $5 per day; one clerk, $2 33; one general foreman, $2 50; one department foreman, $2 16; fourteen gang foremen, $2 58; fifteen machinists, $1 99; nine blacksmiths, $2; eleven blacksmiths' helpers, $1 43; two tinsmiths, $2 73; one helper, $1 40; two stationary engineers, $2; three general laborers, $1 45; one shop sweeper, $1 80; one watchman, $1 66; fourteen painters, $1 50; twenty-eight passenger car builders, $2 25; three upholsterers, $1 07; five passenger car repairers, $2 23; twenty-five freight car repairers, $1 87; twenty-nine truck and box repairers, $1 46; ten car inspectors, $1 54; three car sweepers and cleaners, $1 43. The quantity of work which this department is capable of turning out cannot be estimated from its present force, as it has a much greater capacity than is now needed by the road.

A CHAPTER OF THE IRON AGE.

The rolling mill, a few hundred yards away from the car shop, is a structure of immense size, and as a centre of a vast industry is well worth a visit. The first thing a stranger entering Elmira one of these winter nights observes is the flame-capped chimney which towers above the rolling mill and throws a lurid glare across the widening valley. With the light of dawn the fiery eruption from the chimney pales its ineffectual flame and darkens into a dense cloud of smoke which, borne by the sportive breeze to the distant hills, fills the morning air with all sorts of vapory forms. Under the guidance of Mr. Henry Rathbone, who officiates as high priest in this temple of industry, your correspondent made an inspection of this busy hive of mechanical labor. The uninitiated need a little nerve amid the fiery fragments that come ever and anon thick as a hailstorm from the rolling machines. Dodging the dazzling dangerous lengths of red hot rails and bars which seemed to be running about at random made the time pass in quite a lively and exciting way. And then sauntering through showers of glowing sparks with all the *sang froid* of stoicism of a salamander escaping with three holes in his hat and a severely singed overcoat, the smart of a red hot metallic pellet down his neck, which lodged near the lumber region, and other casualties too numerous to mention, we came from the scene with a vivid remembrance of its primary features. Of course, in passing through this fiery ordeal, the eyes had to do double duty, since the ears were completely deafened by the ceaseless whirring of the mighty wheels turning the ponderous rollers, the wierd humming of the interlacing bands overhead and the fierce roar of the numerous furnaces. Nor could the eyes be trusted altogether, for noticing a pile of iron which seemed to have turned blue from very cold, we approached to take a seat and take notes, but were quickly made to understand the mistake.

First in the line of observation are the "puddlers," who to the number of a dozen or so are puddling away their more or less precious time over huge cauldrons of molten metal, purging it from dross and preparing the residum for manufacturing purposes. "Look out," cries the watchful guide, and while clearing the track for the passage of a number of hand cars loaded with iron bars, the visitor is brought up sharp by the scorching heat from the gaping furnaces. Into the midst of the white heat the black piles of iron go in quick succession, and presently the furnace doors are flung open and out comes the mass glowing like the summer sun. It is then placed on another car, and as it goes blazing through half the length of the shop, like a bright meteor in full combustion, it sends a broad, rich light along the dingy walls and gives the sooty, thickly tangled beams above a glow of golden glory. The strong, black teeth set in the jaws of the resistless rollers seize upon the bright, yellow metal and roll it backwards and forwards as though it were a savory morsel. Now it disappears as if it had been swallowed in the black depths behind but instantly returns, trickling like fiery saliva between the teeth of the rollers. It seems struggling to drag itself away from the power that holds it, but until it is sufficiently attenuated there is no escape. On either side stand lithe and stalworth Vulcans, armed with peculiar tongs, who seize the blazing bar and dexterously toss it to and fro until it has been tortured into the proper shape. It is then allowed to escape on to a long slide, which conducts it within reach of the sharply serrated edges of two rapidly revolving saws, when whiz, crash, and a blinding shower of sparks spring across the wide width of the building. The rail has been cut to the regulation length at both ends, then passes into the open air by easy stages, is inspected, and if found faultless is shoved out of doors into the open air to form a part of the great Erie railway. The rapidity with which this is accomplished is something marvellous, being at the rate of over a rail per minute. The rails are all steel headed and turned out for the use of the Erie Railroad on an average of 20,000 tons a year.

Although not in full blast the Elmira mill gives employment to 350 men, at wages averaging three dollars and fifty cents. The men are paid by the ton, not by the day and expert hands make as much as eight and ten dollars per day.

A POSTSCRIPT OF CONTRADICTIONS.

Mr. Rathbone desired to contradict the statement given out by the Paterson iron workers that Messrs. Fisk and Gould owned and controlled the rolling mill. He says they have an interest in the works but not a controlling one. In reply to the accusation that Fisk and Gould bought a share in order to charge Erie exhorbitant prices for rails, Mr. Rathbone shows by his books that the mills are now supplying rails to the Erie line at a much lower rate than ever before, and this was the object the parties accused had in taking an interest in the concern. Furthermore, he considers that the road was never in such superior order, that its rails will soon be all of steel and its bridges and culverts of iron, and that these statements are but justice to men who really take a live and active interest in rendering the road better than it ever was before.

From the New York Herald, Feb. 6, 1870.

THE ERIE RAILROAD.

OBSERVATIONS HERE AND THERE UPON THE MANAGEMENT—IMPROVEMENTS MADE AND CONTEMPLATED—OPINIONS OF PEOPLE IN THE MATTER—HISTORY OF THE ATLANTIC AND GREAT WESTERN RAILROAD.

BUFFALO, Feb. 2, 1870.

The recent report of Jay Gould on the management of the Erie Railroad, has doubtless given people a clearer idea of the condition of this important line than they possessed previously. Not less instructive was the last strike which has been a positive benefit to the company. It has enabled them to get rid of a class of men who were at all times ready to quit work on some slight pretext or other, and it has demonstrated to all employed, that the present management of the road is not to be trifled with.

As an instance of this spirit the strike of the brakemen and conductors may be instanced. They were swept away and a new class of men employed. In the matter of the conductors a large pecuniary saving was effected—something like $70,000 more than the previous average having been turned into the treasury of the company the month after they were discharged. Some of the conductors, on salaries of $100 per month, lived at the rate of ten thousand a year, had their own handsome houses and horses, and made their nominal wages run wonderfully far. Jim Fisk I believe it was who perceived that a healthy change would be that of exchanging one set of conductors for another, and he did so, with consequences of an eminently satisfactory character. The old conductors, of course, had numerous friends and acquaintances at ever point on the road, and when they were discharged they had many sympathizers, and the road had many enemies.

THE ERIE MANAGEMENT.

The management of the road is a matter which is an important corollary of the late strike. At this particular time, when so much attention is directed to the Erie Railway and the report which Mr. Jay Gould has made excites so much interest by the figures it gives of progress and prosperity, the actual impressions of one who has traveled carefully over the road, stopping at various points, and conversing with people more or less connected with it, may be of advantage in forming an estimate of what this great highway is like and what has been done for it. There is no question that it is vastly improved from what it was three or four years ago, and that its future prospects look brighter day by day. One hundred miles out from Jersey City the traveler, standing at the rear of the train and looking at the track over which he has been rapidily whirled, is reminded of an English railway in the broad, firm and carefully packed road bed, and the high, smooth, solid and unsplintered steel rails. This is one improvement of very material importance—expensive, no doubt, in the start, but cheap and every way more profitable in the long run.

Then, there are the cars, which at one time in the history

of the Erie Railway were mean-looking and very uncomfortable for passengers, but are now certainly equal, if not superior, to those of any other line. There, for instance, is the drawing-room coach already described, which, for luxury on wheels, beats anything that I am acquainted with. You find the station houses are of an improved order. Those at Susquehanna, Elmira and Hornellsville are decidedly fine. Some are of stone, as at the first mentioned place, and, on a small scale, are as luxuriously appointed as the Grand Opera House itself, where the festive Fisk reigns amid the princely surroundings of walnut furniture penciled in gold. The bridges and culverts are being overhauled; iron is taking the place of wood, and the length of the double track is being extended. At this point the Erie suffers one geat drawback in the absence of a passenger depot commensurate with its large and rapidly increasing traffic. Buffalo being one of the principal competing points between the Erie and its principal rivals this is a great disadvantage. Propositions have been made from time to time to construct a grand union depot for the Erie, Lake Shore, and Central roads, and considering that their lines run side by side here this would be an admirable arrangement, and afford every convenience and accommodation to the traveling public. But the Central, being already provided with a pretentious structure, prefers to stand aloof from its dreaded competitor. Nothing remains then, but for Erie to build a depot of its own, and that has been determined upon by the present management. If the plan exhibited to your correspondent be carried out in all its elaborate details the projected depot will be one of the architectural ornaments of this city of magnificent intentions. It will be a broad gauge building *par excellence*, and the waiting rooms will rival the saloon coaches in the magnificence of their appointments. The existing passenger depot is a standing reproach on the old management, and the sooner it is improved upon the sooner the passenger traffic from this point will increase. The workshops at this point are not so extensive as at Jersey City or Susquehanna. They are used for repairing disabled locomotives, passenger and freight cars; but, if necessary, can be adapted to the original conctruction of rolling stock.

There was a time when the road was so reduced in efficiency that it was necessary to buy and borrow engines in different quarters, but now this is all changed. They have ample capacity at Susquehanna to build all the locomotives they need, and they do so, and at Elmira cars are constructed on a scale commensurate with the wants of the company. Here they have a car shop where repairs can be carried on extensively. It is curious to witness the transformation which one of the disabled vehicles of travel undergoes in this department. It may be some poor old passenger car bruised, broken and disfigured all over that to-day comes in to get renovated, and is sent out to-morrow the very counterfeit presentiment of its original self as on the day it first left the hands of the workmen. They wash, scrub and paint it anew, mend the broken places, and take the faded plush seats, and by some process restore the color to a more dazzling crimson than it was originally.

THE TRANSFER OF FREIGHT.

In his report Jay Gould speaks of his arrangements made in exchange of business here with the Lake Shore road. This I find to be the exchange of freight in bulk from the cars of the Lake Shore narrow gauge to those of the Erie board gauge. Hitherto corn from the West when not shipped by canal, went by rail in bags, but now it is brought here in bulk and shovelled quickly from one set of freight cars to the other, as they lay side by side. Another style of transfers is from the boats, of which the Erie Company owns twenty-six, by elevator to the cars. The elevator stands by the river shore, towering up a great height in the air and looking like a dismantled cathedral. Under its ponderous trunk—a good name for the apparatus which dips into the hold of a boat and swallows up the grain—the propellers cast their moorings and discharge their cargoes. The corn disappears from the boat in quick time and drops into freight cars drawn up inside the elevator house. These propellers, twenty-six in number, are each of considerable size, somewhat larger than the steamers between New York and Newburgh. In the season of their usefulness they ply to every place of any importance on the lakes. They reach away up to the mines of Lake Superior and bring down these mountain piles of ore that burden the docks around here. They fetch down everything of a commercial value, and are indeed a great institution, taken collectively. The freight thus brought to the Erie Railroad is something enormous, and to the far-sighted vision of Jay Gould is the road indebted for the addition. Looking around here, first at the geographical position and next at the concentration of lines of communication, it is easy to forecast a great future for Buffalo. The present conception of the Erie Company is to make it a great depot for coal brought from their own mines and shipped by their own boats to a thousand places on the lakes. To do this effectually they have determined to extend their frontage 3,000 feet and increase the depth of water to fifteen feet. Here the boats will draw up, and by an incline plane the cars will be made to carry the coal to an elevation from which it will be shot like a flash of lightning into the awaiting holds below. The improvement under way is of an arduous nature, an immense coffer dam having to be erected and a vast body of water pumped out for the purpose of blasting the rock in the bed of the river.

The freight houses of the Erie Company are large, commodious brick buildings, the principal one being 560 by 200 feet, and well calculated to convey an idea of the immense freight business that flows this way eastward.

OPINIONS OF THE PRESENT MANAGEMENT.

Talking with a gentleman, who was one of the old directors of the Erie road, and has been living here for the past ten years, as to the former management, he said, "the men we had in the direction in my time were a set of barnacles; they let the road run itself, compromised with every kind of strike, and never showed a solitary bit of enterprise. I could see fifty ways of improving the road, but they could see none; they were fossilized. The present management is the best the road ever had, and everybody says so who knows anything about it. Jay Gould has given more time, attention and energy to developing, building and sustaining this road than all the boards of directors that have gone before him. I know this, for I travel over the road very frequently to New York, and can see a great many things he has done for the purpose of benefiting it. He has doubled the supply of rolling stock and doubled the coal traffic. In my time we hardly ever got freight from here to Rochester; now they send 100 cars per day. No effort was made under the old management to compete with the Central at Rochester, and the receipts from passengers reckoned only a few thousand dollars a month; now they count over fifty thousand. On every side I see evidence that great strides have been made towards making Erie what it ought to have been long ago, the great highway of the East, but for the number of sleepy old fossils that had the management; and I think, too, that the people of Albany are standing in their own light in neglecting the chance of incorporating the Albany and Susquehanna Railroad with that of Erie, and sharing in the enterprise that directs it."

Others I have met outside of the men immediately identified with the road, who speak in a similar way, all going to show that no matter what Fisk and Gould may do in Wall street they have done much of substantial service for the Erie Railway.

MISREPRESENTATION OF THE ROAD.

The persistent misrepresentation of the condition and conduct of the Erie road, which certain rival corporations have found it their interest to invent and circulate for the purpose of diverting a portion of the immense business of the great thoroughfare to their own lines, may have influenced such as are far removed and have no opportunity of judging for themselves. In New York the Erie management is more widely known by its connection with the recent gold conspiracy, but here in Buffalo its fame rests principally upon the genius and enterprise of its guiding spirits. "While Drew had charge of the road," remarked a leading flour merchant to your correspondent, "I would not send a single barrel of flour over it, much more risk myself on it. I did my business by the Central, but now that the Erie is in good hands I send all my stuff over it." Pointing to an immense pile of lumber in a yard near the depot, one of the officials of the road remarked. "There sir, is a business which is materially increasing our revenue, and yet it is only about a year since Mr. Gould set about developing it. We had no lumber business at all before his time, and now, though yet in its infancy, it has outgrown our present facilities," and so on. The coal and iron shippers are especially loud in their praise of the present management, as they have been afforded facilities for shipment and transportation they never enjoyed before.

In conclusion, it is fair to say there is nothing strained in the interesting report made by Jay Gould to the stockholders. If he succeed in declaring a dividend one of these fine days everybody will believe him. The report is satisfactory enough, but a dividend would be still more so. His enterprise in securing the carrying trade of the extentive coal region of Carbondale and other points in Pennsylvania redounds vastly to the benefit of the road, and time will prove the correctness and vast pecuniary value of the speculation. When Gould's plans for making the Erie road rich and powerful are matured, he may bid defiance to adverse criticism, for so far he has sufficiently demonstrated the ability to move forward and be successful in spite of almost overwhelming difficulties. The Erie will then no longer be a reproach to New York, but rather the brightest gem in her glittering diadem of grand and noble enterprises.

ATLANTIC AND GREAT WESTERN RAILROAD.

RESUME OF ITS HISTORY — A SPLENDID ENTERPRISE AND ITS EARLY MISMANAGEMENT—VISIONS OF THE PROJECTORS—THE RUIN OF THE ROAD—FISK AND GOULD TO THE RESCUE — FUTURE PROSPECTS.

From the New York Herald, Feb. 6, 1870.

MEADVILLE, Pa., Feb. 4, 1870.

The history of the Atlantic and Great Western Railroad. which has one of its principal stations at this point, furnishes a curious and instructive lesson in commercial enterprises. It was projected under splendid auspices, ten years ago, from the Indian village of Salamanca, on the Erie Railroad, the well-known James McHenry being contractor, foster-father, and finally came near being funeral undertaker. Thomas W. Kennard, who came, it is alleged, to this country with hardly enough means to pay his passage, was chief engineer; but when he severed his connection with the road, he claimed the wealth of a millionaire. The stockholders hailed from England, and among them figured Sir Morton Peto, who freely unlocked the fountains of his treasure, and poured it into the new enterprise, which the dauntless McHenry undertook to carry through. High hopes accompanied it. Visions of grasping the whole trade of the West, North-west and South-west, the lakes, the Mississippi, and finally the Pacific coast, floated before the fancy of the projectors, while just as it was started came the wildly exciting intelligence that oil of precious properties was springing like a fountain of living waters from the soil almost directly in the path of its progress. An immense force of men was placed upon the work, and it was hurried forward under the inspiring genius of McHenry at as rapid a pace as the Union Pacific. English capital was lavished upon it as capital was never lavished before. Here at Meadville a station was put up rivalling, in the style and beauty of its surroundings, any of those you may notice in the best railroads in England; charming cottages for the officers of the road; a park at the rear, with winding walks, fir trees, rose and jessamine bushes. A hotel of over 100 rooms, and a dining-room as long as a train of freight cars were a portion of the grand enterprise. In the fall of 1862 the road reached here, after creating two towns, named Corry and Jamestown, on its way from Salamanca. It was pushed steadily along—broad gauge all the way to Dayton—and from there, by laying down a third rail on another road to Cincinnati, ultimately reached the Queen City of the West—striking the Ohio and aiming for the Mississippi. A branch called the Franklin was built from here to Oil City, and another from Braceville to Cleveland. The region of flowing petroleum was tapped at the opportune moment, and by way of the line to Cleveland the oil was carried to the refineries. Looking over the railroad map, which represents one contiguous broad gauge road, extending from New York first by the Erie, then by Atlantic and Great Western to Cincinnati, you will readily admit that the visions of James McHenry and his confiding English friends were none too sanguine. How much more exalted might the British fancy have become had the two roads at that time been of the one construction and management, the Erie stretching to the lakes through the great State of New York, and lapping its branches around the richest coal beds of Pennsylvania, while the Atlantic drew off the abundant and exhaustless riches of the oil region! Such is the state of affairs now, but it was not reserved for McHenry to be the instrument of its realization. The road started out with really magnificient prospects. It opened up a new and wonderfully rich region; it struck for the carrying trade of the mighty West; it infused a quickening growth into the old and fossilized towns through which it passed, building up an important local traffic and directing a fresh current of commerce towards the State of New York.

Notwithstanding all this the road failed to prosper, and went steadily down until the beginning of the year 1869. Grossly corrupt and inefficient management brought this splendid highway to a condition of reproach. The directors and others identified with it appear to have shown a strange lack of energy and foresight when a little of either might have rescued the concern from the verge of bankruptcy at which it had arrived. The present management of Erie, which succeeded in saving that road from bankruptcy or absorption by that hardy mariner, the much-bronzed Vanderbilt, is the only one it seems to me, that can bring back the prestige and carry out the destiny of the Atlantic and Great Western Railroad.

WHAT THE ROAD CREATED.

That this destiny is one of vast import may be seen by a brief study of the map. The first station of note after leaving Salamanca is Jamestown. It is situated at the head of the rapids at the outlet of Chautaque Lake, New York State. Two steamers ply to Mayville, a station on what is called the Cross Cut Railroad. Vast quantities of lumber are floated down to Jamestown, and from thence sent by rail or river in various directions. Jamestown was created by the Atlantic and Great Western road less than ten years ago, and is a lively, bustling town. The next place of importance is Corry, a similar creation to the one already mentioned, but of larger and more earnest growth. It is the terminus of the Oil Creek Railroad, the Brocton Cross Cut Railroad, and the crossing point of the Philadelphia and Erie Railroad. It has railroad communication in five different directions, and will shortly have a sixth. It has large machine shops, woollen, and hardware factories, three national banks and seven churches; yet twelve years ago, it was a dreary wilderness. Next comes Meadville, an old village, lingering for years in venerable vegetation, but, touched by the magnetism of the railroad, bloomed into willing freshness and prosperity. It has factories, banks, and colleges, and a population of about 12,000 inhabitants. A line of boats run to Pittsburg and to Erie, on the lake by the Erie Canal, of which the Venango River is the feeder at this point. West of here are other towns on the line of the Atlantic and Great Western, which have been either called into existence, or impelled to prosperous expansion by the road.

ONE WAY OF ROBBING THE ROAD STOPPED.

It should be understood that before the projection of the line this section of Pennsylvania was a comparative *terra incognita*, its resources unknown and means of communication rude and primative in the last degree. The measure of development it has received through the agency of this railroad cannot be adequately gauged by figures, but that the railroad itself should have failed to reap the reward for the benefits it conferred is a question which resolves itself into the simple solutation that its management was extravagant and incompetent. I heard a good joke at Salamanca going to illustrate the light in which the former conductors on this road viewed the change of management, which occurred over a year ago. The road had depreciated so much, its receipts had diminished so low, that it went into the hands of two receivers, one of whom was Jay Gould. The latter set to work with his accustomed energy, and pursued the same plan of action in striving to resuscitate the fallen fortunes of the Atlantic which he had previously used in the case of Erie. He saw one leak in the receipts was the stealings of the conductors, and according to all accounts these were notoriously wholesale. Whether American prejudice to many things English got the better of their conscience or not, certain it is the conductors indulged an easy swing of the passenger receipts and made a beggarly show to the treasurer. "Now I don't see why Jay Gould should have discharged us," observed an ex-conductor shortly after his dismissal, "for if we had not knocked down the stamps as we did he would never have been made receiver."

The doings of the conductors, detrimental as they were to the pecuniary interests of the road, were but a trifle compared with those of officials higher in authority. United to extravance in almost every department was a total absence of enterprise or effort towards arresting the downward progress of the concern, and hence a receiver was appointed, and hence it was that English capitalists bewailed their American experience. But there was really never a better prospect before the road than there is now, and a year or so will certainly prove that the wisest thing its stockholders eve did was to lease it to the Erie line and let the two be consolidated under one vigorous management. Time will show that the destiny of these lines and that of the Ohio and Missisippi, the three being of the broad gauge width, is to reach from the Atlantic to the Father of Waters in unbroken union and under a single direction.

THE DIVISIONS OF THE LINE AND ITS TRAFFIC.

The Atlantic and Great Western is made up of five divisions—first, from Salamanca to Meadville; second, from Meadville to Kent; third, from Kent to Gallion; fourth, from Gallion to Dayton, and fifth, from Mahoning branch, which now extends from New Lisbon to Cleveland, and has a spur running out to Sharon. Each of these has a superintendent, and then a general one for all, who resides here—Mr. O. S. Lyford. Mr. L. D. Rucker was formerly general superintendent for a term of two years. He introduced an administration of economy which proved very distasteful to many of the old employes, who remembered the halcyon days when the princely Peto and his party of reputed millionaires journeyed over the line and said everything looked lovely, though their money had been squandered or buried in the roadbed over which they rolled. The branches or feeders of the line are numerous and increasing in number. The one from Oil City to Corry brings the crude petroleum in tanks for shipment over the Atlantic and Erie to New York. The Mahoning branch to Cleveland is almost exclusively an oil route, and supplies the refineries in Cleveland with the crude oil from the wells. The importance of a freight like this, the bulk of which is every year increasing, cannot be overestimated. Petroleum is not about to give out, as the popular anticipation would have it, but will continue to form one of our great and permanent staples of export, even as cotton and grain do. The oil trade is one heavy item of traffic on the Atlantic line, next coal, then grain, and lastly general merchandise. The through passenger traffic has greatly increased since the consolidation with Erie. The local traffic is considerable. The increase of 1869 over 1868 on the Erie line is, according to the President's report, 302,765 passengers, and this, in a great measure, is due to the consolidation. The freight traffic of the Erie shows an increase in 1869 over 1867 of 787,216 tons. Next year will probably exceed this figure by a quarter of a million and the year after by over half a million. To this prosperity the Atlantic and Great Western Railroad has contributed no inconsiderable share. As a passenger route from New York to Chicago and Cincinnati it makes with the Erie one unbroken broad gauge track to the latter city and Cleveland.

THE PRESENT MANAGEMENT.

The Atlantic and Great Western was leased by the Erie company 1st of January, 1869, for one year, and has now been leased again by the same company on "substantially the same terms as of the original lease." The rolling stock of the Erie operates on the other road along with that of its own. The Atlantic and Great Western road was wretchedly provided with freight and passenger cars and owned but a limited number of locomotives. The Erie motive power is now used extensively from one end of the road to the other. The station houses on the line from Salamanca here are good, the trains make excellent time and the roadbed is improved very much from what it was a few years ago. The future before it is vast and only needs a clear-headed management to make it certain of attainment. Talking to a gentleman to-day on the prospects of the line, said he, "If they will only leave it in its present hands the Atlantic and Great Western will be one of the first roads in the country. They may talk as they please about these men, Fisk and Gould, but you've got to fight the devil with fire. You've got to fight Vanderbilt, Drew and such men with their own weapons, and it's all a waste of talk to say a road like this can be made what it ought to be without raising a hue and cry in some quarters." But it is necessary to penetrate the oil regions before saying more about the great resources upon which the road may rely for support.

OPINIONS ON THE PRESS.

The New York papers having paid such particular attention to the affairs of the Erie Railway Corporation, and differed so widely in their conclusions, the following remarks may enable the reader to decide as to which are the more independent and impartial of our leading daily Journals.

HERALD.

First and foremost comes the *Herald*—the most independent, liberal and enterprising journal in the World. Fearless alike in praising or blaming, as evidenced in its treatment of the Erie managers. It was the first to censure Gould and Fisk for their share in the Corbin & Co.'s celebrated gold corner, and it was among the first to give them credit for the wonderful energy and ability displayed, and the marvelous success they have achieved, in the management of the Erie road. It has refrained from condemning the Erie officials of "abusing trusts," "misappropriating funds," etc., etc., for the simple but sufficient reason that their accusers have not yet been able to substantiate any one of the many serious charges, from time to time, circulated through the medium of subsidised journals. But when the Messrs. Gould, Fisk, Lane, *et al.*, render the account of their stewardship of the finances of the Corporation, which is now in course of preparation, that statement will undergo no closer, keener, or more impartial scrutiny, item by item, than at the council board presided over by the Nestor of American journalism—and, commendation or condemnation, the Erie officials will be rewarded according to their deserts.

The columns of the *Herald* will be searched in vain for anything like the gratuitous abuse and shameless slanders which the *Times* and *Tribune*, conspicuous among all other journals, have published in the interests of the enemies of Erie.

In view of what Messrs. Gould and Fisk have already done in the way of increasing the business facilities of the road under their care, and of what they have determined to do in order to establish a through line for the produce of the far West, it would seem that these men, of all others, have profited most by the teachings of the *Herald*, which has ever been the advocate of national enterprise, and the pioneer of American progress. And yet, the time was when the *Herald*, now acknowledged the leading paper in the World for enterprise, and equally well entitled to the proud distinction of being the only really independent organ of public opinion, occupied a similar position in the world of journalism to that the Erie Company fills to-day in the railway world. It was a journalistic Ishmael. A war of annihilation was waged against it by a band of powerful rivals, and, receiving no quarter, it could not afford to give any. At that time its indomitable editor had as good a claim to the unenviable distinction of being one of the best abused men in the country as Fisk or Gould have now. To-day, in his nobly earned prosperity, Mr. Bennett's friends are legion, but how few and far between were those who had the courage to stand by him during the long years in which he so bravely battled through trouble to triumph.

As yet, the *Herald* has done nothing more than to demand fair play for the accused; it has cautiously abstained from rendering anything in the way of "aid and comfort," until the production of satisfactory evidence that the persons associated in the present management of Erie are really the good and faithful servants they claim to be. With the bitter experiences of the dark days of his own eventful and marvelous career in mind, it may be that the aged veteran, who, while reposing from his life-labor, enjoys the pleasure of watching the straightforward and fearless course of the young journalist, to whom he has relinquished the helm, feels something like sympathy for the daring spirits who so boldly undertook the apparently hopeless task of defending the shattered craft Erie from the mutinous directors, who had conspired to scuttle it, the pirate monopolists who were bent on capture and plunder, and the hungry horde of Wall-street speculators who were in hope of stealing something from the wreck. While being so skillfully navigated through the financial dangers which encompassed it and periled its existence, the good ship Erie has been thoroughly repaired, refitted, and rendered seaworthy, and it is to be hoped it will yet forge ahead of its rivals, and rank A 1, like its journalistic prototype. Having survived so much, Gould and Fisk will undoubtedly live down the malice of their opponents, and command respect and admiration throughout the length and breadth of a land benefitted by the reresults of their genius, enterprise, and all-conquering energy. So mote it be.

THE ERIE REPORT.

From the N. Y. Tribune, Jan. 21, 1870.

Alaska has a tropical climate, and strawberries in their season. The Borgia was a saintly, much-slandered martyr of a woman. The Devil is white. Mr. Jay Gould shows, in other columns, how admirable, successful, and economical is his management of the Erie Railway.

Here and now, we prefer to utter no dissent. We leave Mr. Gould's report to speak for itself;—only commending it to the earnest attention of those bewildered stockholders who cannot quite understand why so prosperous a concern doesn't pay any dividends.

Meanwhile we venture to place beside Mr. Gould's glowing exhibit, another statement. Some forty or fifty law suits and supplementary proceedings are pending against the Erie Railway Company, or rather against Messrs. Gould, Fisk, and Lane, its officers and managers. It is a point worth considering. In these cases various allegations and charges are made under the solemnity of an oath, some of them of the most grave and serious nature, affecting character and integrity. These gentlemen are openly charged with having made wholesale issues of Erie shares and bonds, and with having misappropriated the moneys derived therefrom, as well as having taken the entire earnings of this great line of railway without accounting therefor, except in payment of running expenses and in meeting the interest and lease obligations of the company.

These charges are either true *or false.* The persons thus accused are either *honest men, striving with their best ability to manage the affairs of the company for the benefit of its stockholders*, or they are swindlers, actively engaged in stealing money which belongs to others. We do not seek now to judge between the parties, Messrs. Fisk, Gould, and Lane *have a right to be heard in their defense, and should not be condemned in advance of trial.* But the gravity of the charges seems clearly to demand more than a rose-colored official report. Mr. Gould can have these written by the dozen, in far better style than the present one, with half as many facts and twice as good a showing, for less than the cost of one injunction. We speak plainly. The affairs of Erie have come to such a pass that neither the stockholders nor the public believe a statement authenticated by the signature of its officers. The charges made can only be set at rest by a thorough judicial investigation; *and we cannot see why these gentlemen should not themselves court it.* If the moneys received have been honestly appropriated for the benefit of the company, there can be no serious difficulty in making that fact appear; and it seems due to themselves, due to the Erie stockholders, to the holders of other railway shares, and to the public, that these gentlemen promptly submit themselves to the test of a trial. *If they have been falsely accused the odium will rest upon the accusers; they will put their enemies to shame and stand exonerated before the public.* Why not, then, permit some of these suits to be fairly tried? If Mr. Ramsey has made false charges against Fisk & Co., let them be disproved judicially, and let Mr. Ramsey take the consequences. The opponents of the Erie managers aver that they dare not risk the chances of a judicial investigation; that they are averse to being cross-examined in open court, and that all their legal measures are intended to delay or postpone indefinately, by money influence or otherwise, suits which threaten to bring them to a reckoning with the long-suffering stockholders.

We do not now make these charges. We do say that if Messrs. Gould & Co. desire the public to accept and believe them, they could hardly find a more effective way of accomplishing that result than by resorting to subterfuge in order to evade an early and fair trial of the main issue involved.

Reports, gentlemen, will not answer the purpose. What is wanted is *Trial!*

The foregoing is really an excellent specimen of the meaningless mixture of Bunsbyism and bile with which a certain member of the editorial staff of the *Tribune* is allowed to serve up his hermaphroditical opinions. The three startling statements with which the article opens are so entirely foreign to the subject in hand that one is at a loss to account for their abrupt introduction. Can it be that the writer indulged in them by way of consolation for the obviously distaseful duty of admitting that Mr. Gould's Report "shows how admirable, successful, and economical is his management of the Erie Railway." Is it possible that the naked truth is so unpalatable as to require a treble coating of mendacity to enable one pungent pill to pass the editorial gorge? Alas, it would really seem so—otherwise, what motive could there be for the promulgation of such a palpable fiction as that concerning the climate of Alaska? Why, Mr. Seward himself did not go as far as strawberries in enumerating the "fruits" of that frozen waste. That Lucretia Borgia was "a saintly much-slandered martyr of a women" is somewhat contrary to the opinion hitherto entertained of that not much lamented lady. Yet, it may have been so. This statement however would be much easier of belief were it supported by one (equally probable) to the effect that the Borgia's saintly reputation was ruined by the persistent misrepresentations of the licentious press of the period. Apologists for his Satanic Majesty have repeatedly declared that Lucifer's complexion is much lighter than the conventional lamp-black in which it is customary to portray him, but the *Tribune* goes the length of saying: "The Devil is white." Well, its no use being particular as to a shade. Some people will insist upon it that black is white, and *vice versa,* and in the event of the editor being mistaken on this comparatively unimportant point let us be charitable and hope he may yet have an opportunity of discovering, if not of recanting his error.

In preferring to "utter no dissent," and leaving Mr. Gould's report to speak for itself the *Tribune* does wisely and well. In commending it to the attention of the stockholders the editor puts himself to unneccessary trouble—the document commends itself.

After setting forth the accusations made against Messrs. Gould, Fisk & Lane *et al*, the Bunsby of the *Tribune* edifies his readers with the following solid chunk of wisdom: "These charges are either true *or* false." If not, why so? We are next informed that "the persons thus accused are either honest men, striving with their best ability to manage the affairs of the company for the benefit of the stockholders, *or* they are swindlers, actually engaged in stealing money which belongs to others." Just so! and wherefor because? Well, by a similar token, it may be as boldly advanced that the "officers of the *Tribune* Association are either honest men, striving with their best ability to further the interests of the proprietors, or they are a pack of swindlers actively engaged in endeavoring to conceal their manifold sins against the ten commandments. And also, that the writer of the article under treatment, is either a knave, a fool, or a sensible and conscientious journalist. If so be as how, why then? Sauce for the goose is sauce for the gander.

Cognizant that "some forty or fifty law suits and supplementary proceedings are pending against the Erie Railway Company, or rather against Messrs. Gould, Fisk & Lane, its officers and managers," the *Tribune* "cannot see why these gentlemen should not themselves court" additional litigation of a hostile nature. May it not be that the Erie managers are sensible enough to confine their efforts to combatting the ills they have, instead of pursuing the suicidal policy of meeting trouble half-way?

In conclusion, the editor rules that the accused "have a right to be heard in their defence, and should *not* be condemned in advance of trial." The existence of a doubt is admitted, but the "impartial" journalist seems exceeding loath to give the Erie managers the benefit. However, in clamoring for a trial the *Tribune* acknowledges that no proof of guilt has yet been established, and, this more or less influential sheet being so notoriously destitute of anything like *moral* conviction, must perforce allow presumptive innocence.

It would be unjust, however, to condemn the entire editorial staff for the faults and follies of any one writer, and prominent among the honorable exceptions in the present instance is Mr. Greeley himself. Some paragraphs, written much in the style of the article on Mr. Gould's Report, appeared in the *Tribune* a few weeks ago, charging the Erie managers with complicity in what was alleged to be an attempt to murder a certain member of the legal profession. A demand for a retraction of these infamous insinuations was insolently refused by one of the subordinate editors; but no sooner was Mr. Greeley's attention called to the matter, than the wrong so maliciously perpetrated, was promptly confessed and editorially atoned for.

TIMES.

The *N. Y. Times* has, perhaps, done more for the Vanderbilt interest, in the past, than any other journal, and, consequently, has been particularly inimical to the present managers of Erie. The gentleman who holds the responsible position of financial editor of this once impartial and influential sheet, is credited with the authorship of the more slanderous of the many unjust and inconsiderate articles it has published for the especial benefit of combinations antagonistic to the best interests of the Erie Corporation, and to the detriment of American credit abroad. An open and avowed enemy of Messrs. Gould and Fisk, this gentleman enjoyed the immense advantage of being able to manipulate one of the leading organs of public opinion, and make it the engine of his personal hostility—an advantage of which he did not scruple to avail himself. Quite recently, however, it has been discovered that it does not pay to allow contributors, however old and valuable, to make use of the paper as a vehicle for private animosities, and our financial friend, who so long had "full swing," is now so restricted that though he "nothing extenuates," he is not permitted to set down ought in malice. This is a great improvement, and the *Times* will undoubtedly be as much benefitted thereby as the Erie management. Being the recognized English organ, this paper is of course bound to support the British financiers who are now filibustering for the control of the great highway of the American continent.

SUN.

The *Sun*, as its appropriate motto truthfully asserts, "shines for all," and is in many respects a bright example to its more pretentious and less impartial cotemporaries. While giving full publicity to all complaints against the Erie managers—no matter whence they may emanate, from the Jersey City strikers, Wall-street speculators, or the Ramsey-Eaton Vanderbilt ring, the accused have also had the benefit of its enormous and ever-growing circulation for such defence as they might put forward.

WORLD.

Although the first to publish a plea for Erie, the *World* was the first paper to give aid and comfort to the English triumvirate, Messrs. Raphael, Heath and Bischoffschiem, who, under the shallow pretence of championing the rights of the foreign stockholders, have conspired with the managers of rival American lines against the best interests of the Erie stockholders generally. It is rumored that in securing the services of Mr. S. L. M. Barlow, as one of his counsel, Mr. Burt, the emissary of the pretended Protection Committee, secured the influence of the *World*. In all the other contests in which the Erie management have been engaged, the leading Democratic organ has advocated fair play, and it is not yet so far committed to Mr. Barlow's British patrons as to preclude the possibility of retreating with honor.

THE ENGLISH PROTECTION SCHEME EXPLODED.

JAY GOULD IN DEFENCE OF THE AMERICAN MANAGEMENT.

Mr. Charles Burt, a British barrister, having appeared before the Senate Railroad Committee, at Albany, and, with the insolent assumption of superiority which is such an objectionable characteristic of the majority of his countrymen who condescend to visit this benighted country, coolly demanded that the laws of the Empire State should be immediately altered for the exclusive benefit of a clique of London stock-jobbers, Mr. Jay Gould, the President of the Erie Railroad Company, presented himself before the same committee on the 23d of March, and made the following able and unanswerable argument against the repeal of the so-called Erie Bill:

Gentlemen:—In replying to the charges made against the present management of the Erie Railway by one who claims to represent a large majority of stockholders resident in England, I shall state only such facts as are capable of the clearest proof, as I deem this course the best for the cause of truth and justice, and calculated to carry conviction to the minds of all who hear me, of the utter groundlessness of the accusations against me and my associates, so boldly made before this Committee.

First. I claim that the real clients of Mr. Burt are two Jewish bankers (Heath & Raphael); that the money to carry on the proceeding was obtained by coercion and fraud, and that Mr. Burt represents only a small minority of *bona fide* owners of Erie stock, viz., Robert A. Heath, 1,100 shares; Heath and Raphael, 3,500 shares; Raphael & Sons, 56,400 shares. Total, $6,100,000. Letters from London stockholders have been received, protesting against the proceedings of the Committee. I and another gentleman own two millions of Erie Stock, which we are carrying in London. I was compelled, by a resolution of the

London Stock Exchange, to have it stamped, and pay a shilling per share to Mr. Burt's Committee to fight myself. Now this Committee propose to go a step further, and compel me, if I expect to carry my stock in Lordon or have it merchantable at the London Stock Exchange, to register that stock in the name of Heath & Raphael—by a resolution of the London Stock Exchange, that no certificate of Erie stock shall be a good delivery except it is registered in the name of these gentlemen. Comprehend for a moment the result of this proposition. You condense in the hands of two gentlemen the entire voting power of the Erie Railway stock, while it is actually owned by 2,000 different individuals. Of this stock Messrs. Heath & Raphael need not own one dollar. *Bona fide* owners are to have no voice, and the Board of Directors to manage the affairs and administer to the wants of this great corporation is to be made up in the dingy office of a Jew banking-house in London. It seems to me that such a condition of things is the most conclusive argument of the wisdom of the law. By this judicious enactment the control of the road is prevented from passing into the hands of inexperienced and irresponsible parties, and it is effectually secured from been sold out to the Pennsylvania Central or the New York Central Companies, either of which could well afford to pay two millions or three millions to shut up or localize the Erie. So much for the origin and object of the London movement.

Second. With regard to the statements made by Mr. Burt before your committee, I can only say that they conflict with expressions used both in conversation with myself and in the hearing of others. When it became known that Mr. Burt had arrived in New York, I took immediate steps to afford him every facility for an examination of the Company's affairs. I obtained the services of an influential gentleman, who called on Mr. Burt in my interest and made to him, at my request, the most friendly and conciliatory advances, offering to take him over the line and show him the actual condition of the Company's property and the working of the departments. Mr. Burt, however, refused to hold any intercourse with Erie Directors until the demands of Messrs. Raphael & Co. were fully satisfied. I naturally felt hurt at such rude and uncourteous treatment, and determined to allow matters to take their course without further interference. Shortly afterward, Mr. Burt apparently ashamed of the position he had at first taken, sent a message to me requesting a personal interview and asking me to call upon him. It seemed to me that this was a little more than he deserved, considering the spirit in which he had received my advances. But feeling anxious to harmonize any difference between us, and willing to do all in my power to assist in arriving at a settlement of the question at issue in the controversy, I complied with his request, and our interview took place accordingly. To relate all that occurred between us on that occasion would tax my memory and your patience more than would be either pleasant or profitable. Some observations and admissions of Mr. Burt's may, however, be repeated here. He approved of the principle of classification as embodied in the Director's bill, and remarked that a similar provision was in force on many English railroads. He spoke in very flattering terms of myself and Mr. Fisk, going so far as to pronounce us the ablest railroad managers in this country, and stating his wish that we should remain in the Board of Directors. He demanded, on behalf of those he represented, that he should have the nomination and selection of twelve out of the seventeen directors, and hinted at his own appointment as Treasurer. I asked him to name the parties whom he wished to include in the list of directors, and would use my influence to have them substituted for an equal number now in the Board. I also offered to resign my place as Treasurer, saying I should be glad to have some good responsible man to carry on the finances of the road as I had been doing, first, however, reimbursing the amounts I had advanced to the Company during my term of office. To these propositions, however, I could get no intelligible reply, and soon afterward the interview was closed. It remains for Mr. Burt to reconcile, as best he can, the statements made to me and those uttered before your Committee.

Third. As to the Classification bill, the repeal of which Mr. Burt so loudly demands, I would say that it is, according to his own admission, by no means unknown in England. The principle of classifying railroad directors, so that only a small proportion of the whole number would relinquish office each year, was first introduced in the United States on the Illinois Central Railroad. It has been gradually extended, and is now the law in most of the States. The reasons for such a law are obvious, its tendency being to furnish an experienced and competent management beyond the control of speculative influences. The only objection made to the law was that it did not in the first instance allow the stockholders to vote.

Previous to the last annual election, however, the old Board of Directors voted to invite an expression of opinion by the stockholders, as to the expediency of adopting the classification. A meeting was accordingly held of all or a large majority of the stockholders, and a resolution adopted directing the new Board to classify its members in accordance with the provisions of the Director's bill. In this way, I submit, the only objection ever made to this enactment by the press, either of this country or of England, has been removed. Mr. Burt does not represent a single share of stock that has not approved of this bill, When the law was passed, only a small minority of the stock of the Erie Railway Company was held in England. Messrs. Raphael & Co., have purchased their stock since the passage of the law, with full knowledge of its existence and approval of its provisions. If, as Mr. Burt says, he represents a majority of the stock by an ownership acquired in a few months, held by foreigners having no sympathy with the growth or development of this country, whose manufactories and great iron interests are in direct antagonism to ours, and whose money is freely subscribed and lavishly spent in their National Legislature to cripple and destroy the manufactures of this country, what more effectual method could they employ than to send over a batch of Englishmen to run the Erie Road, under importers' restrictions, that would crush out every manufactory on the line of the road? In this way a blow could be struck which would do irreparable injury before the mischief could be remedied.

Fourth: With regard to mismanagement and extravagance on the Erie Railway. Now, gentlemen, Mr. Burt makes a broad assertion in this matter, but does not choose to point out any particular department in which there is a want of economy. He does not furnish either facts or figures, nor does he present the opinion of a single practical railroad man to sustain this charge. He has not visited the line where he could have conversed with the inhabitants and ascertained their opinions as to the efficacy of the management. I am the more surprised at this, because Mr. Burt, in a conversation with myself and another gentleman, expressed entirely different views, as I have already had occasion to state. Gentlemen, we took charge of the Erie Railway in July 1868, less than two years ago. At that time it was fast becoming localized. The gross earnings had declined from $16,426,000 in 1865, to $14,376,000 in 1867, a loss of over $2,000,000. We have brought the earnings up to $16,500,000 the past year. When we assumed control of the road the property had been allowed to deteriorate, and the traveling public had lost confidence in the road. Now, the fine condition of the line is the theme of universal comment, while the luxury of our cars is spoken of by travelers as surpassing any rival route. In the matter of economy, I would say that there are three great elements which enter into the operating expenses of a railroad, namely, fuel, iron, and steel, and labor. With regard to the first, the cost in 1866 for fuel per mile run on the Erie Railway was 24 cents, and at the present time our fuel costs us only about 13 cents per mile run, a very important saving, when it is considered that we run about eight millions of miles annually. This saving is the result of using coal instead of wood, the Company owning mines from which they can obtain their supply for many years to come, thus saving all intermediate profits. As to the second item of expenditure, we manufacture our iron and steel rails at our own mills, under the most rigid inspection as to strenght and quality, believing that in this department especially, the best is always the cheapest. We have reduced the cost of manufacture since we took the road $10 per ton on steel, and $5 per ton on iron, besides securing rails that will wear twice the length of time that those originally used would last. There remains for special notice the item of labor, which enters very largely into all calculations of the cost of operating railroads; and thinking that reliable statistics would not fail to interest you, I have had estimates prepared, showing the amount of the gross earnings of the past three months, together with the amount paid for labor during the same period, as compared with the three corresponding months of the preceeding year, as follows:

GROSS EARNINGS.		AMOUNT OF PAY-ROLL.	
December, 1868,...	$1,199,309 88	December, 1868,...	$530,530 14
January. 1869, ...	1,147,685 15	January, 1869,....	514,623 12
February, 1869, ...	998,793 74	February, 1869,...	486,059 50
Total,........	$3,345,788 77	Total,.........	$1,531,212 76
December, 1869,...	$1,170,891 00	December, 1869, ..	$487,367 12
January, 1870, ...	1,140,748 00	January, 1870,....	428,756 72
February, 1870, ...	1,061,311 00	February, 1870,...	408,632 25
Total, ...	$3,372,950 00	Total,.........	$1,324,756 09
Increase in earnings,	$27,161 23	Decreas'd cost labor,	$206,456 67

Gentlemen, I have now laid before you the facts and statements which fully meet every accusation of Mr. Burt and expose the slight foundations on which his charges are based. Permit me to thank you, gentlemen, for the patience with which you have indulged me, and allow me to ask your indulgence for a few moments while I offer some suggestions as to the true policy of the State Legislature dealing with the great avenues of transportation, and the vast interests with which they are connected. The completion of the Erie Canal marked an era in the prosperity, not only of the City of New York, but of the whole State. The products of the Great West found an easy channel of communication with the seaboard, and the position of New York as a great commercial and financial center was from that date secure. As time passed on, however, the canal was found to be inadequate to transport the immense and increasing productions of the new States of the North-West, and a year after witnessed the construction and expose of our railroads whose vast network now covers the face of the country; and now came the struggle for the carrying trade, and rival lines strained every nerve to obtain the lion's share of the lucrative traffic. What wonder, then, that in this eager strife between the railroad interests, the canal should have been comparatively neglected, as, both in capacity and speed of transit, it was outstripped by the more modern method of transportation. It has transpired that a project is on foot to improve the revenue of the canal by legislation contemplating a reduction of tolls in order to compete with railroads. I would most respectfully urge upon the Legislature the policy of "letting well enough alone." There should be, in my judgment, no conflict between the canal and railroads. The teeming west, as yet but partially developed, will furnish business sufficient for every avenue of communication at remunerative rates, and the people of the State of New York whose means were so freely contributed for the construction of the Erie Canal, be assured a fair return for their investment. There is ample proof of the fact that in every struggle for supremacy between the canals and railroads, the canals were invariably the sufferers. Let the experience of the past point out our true policy in this matter, and once more let me say, "Let well enough alone." One more suggestion, and I have done. It should not be lost sight of that Philadelphia and Baltimore are rivals of New York, and that they are 100 miles nearer the Great West by rail than New York is. If, therefore, the commerce of our great city is to be sustained and protected, we must overcome this disadvantage in distance by every means in our power, although in this effort we are compelled to materially lessen the charge of transportation.

A BRITISH COUNTER-BLAST TO BURT.

Mr. George Crouch, an Anglo-American stockholder, next addressed the Committee on behalf of the English shareholders, who protested against the scheme of Messrs. Raphael & Co. Mr. Crouch said:

My excuse for trespassing on your time is something similar to that of Mr. Burt. I own 5,000 shares of Erie stock in England, and in addition I represent the shares of a number of correspondents there, who protest against the scheme of which Mr. Burt's clients (Raphael & Co.) are the prime movers. I would say, by way of preface to my demurrers to Mr. Burt's plea, that while connected with a leading New York journal, I had an opportunity of obtaining an insight into the operations and affairs of the Erie Railway Company, in consequence of which, I was applied to by friends in England for further information. I then called upon the President of the road for such information, expecting that it would be denied me, but I was agreeably surprised to find that, on the contrary, every facility was given. I was allowed to inspect the books as far as I wanted, and to examine the road itself. In fact, I had every opportunity to obtain the information I desired. That information was published here very extensively, and no point in it has been denied, although it contradicted nearly every charge that has been made as to the business and condition of the road. On the papers in which it appeared reaching England, the parties whom I now represent concluded to hold their stock as long as there was any prospect of the present management remaining in control. Apprehending the worst possible consequences for all parties in the interest from the action of the self-constituted Protective Committee, a number of prominent holders on the other side have placed their shares under my control, instructing me to make protest in their behalf. To-day I speak in behalf of $2,000,000 worth of Erie stock, owned in England, and I am advised that within a very short time there will be a much more serious reduction in the number of shares Messrs. Raphael & Co. are now striving to control. The partial insurrection of the foreign stockholders of Erie is one of the last, but by no means the least, disastrous, of the many evils which have resulted to all parties interested, from the reprehensible measures adopted by the enemies of the present management. Disappointed at the failure of their individual and united efforts, the Ramsey-Eaton-Vanderbilt party in their determination to be revenged in some way or other, finally hit upon the bright idea of using the English interest as a cats-paw. Their plans in this connection were admirably well laid, and so far successful at the outset as to raise the most sanguine hopes of obtaining almost immediate possession of the long-coveted chestnuts. Ignorant alike of the history, condition and prospects of the road, and, most obvious point of all, ignorant of the ulterior designs of the eontemptible conspirators who are stirring them up to mutiny against the best managers Erie ever had. A very considerable number of the foreign stockholders have been shamefully imposed upon by the agents of rival American corporations, and the would be successors of Gould and Fisk. The most tempting bait, however, was the prospect of ousting the American directors and filling their places with Englishmen. Thanks to that dazling delusion, the London stockholders did not perceive the hook on which they are now suspended until they had been bled by the philanthropic financiers who compose the so called "Protective Committee," to the tune of £25,000. They see the hook now, and feel it; but they will be bled pretty dry before they are allowed to wriggle off. Their confidence in the protestations and promises of the men to whom they so foolishly intrusted their shares will be somewhat rudely shaken when they learn that Mr. Burt, while pleading, as he says, in their behalf before the Senate Railway Committee in Albany, said: "If we could have the opportunity to-morrow of appointing a board of directors of this Company, we should *not* appoint men who live in London, or men who would look simply to the interests of the shareholders in England." No better illustration of the sublime imprudence with which the English shareholders resident on the other side have been imposed upon from time to time by their American friends, is needed than the fact that they were actually bamboozled into the belief that Drew and Vanderbilt fought the great fight of 1868 for the benefit of the stockholders generally, and the English interest particularly.

Absurd as this preposterous belief must appear to such as have even the slightest knowledge of the case, it was nevertheless fondly entertained by the majority of the foreign stockholders, until a few weeks ago, when in order to persuade them to subscribe for the furtherance of the schemes of the English "Protectors," it was found necessary to dissipate the delusion concerning their American "friends." Much surprise and no little indignation was manifested when Mr. Raphael, the head center of the "Protection Ring," told the British shareholders that "it had been pointed out to the committee that the actions brought against the Erie directors by Mr. Drew and Mr. Vanderbilt and others, had been instigated for private purposes, and that they (Drew and Vanderbilt) were so far satisfied with the result, they had attained ($5,000,000 worth of plunder), that the law suits had been allowed to drop. No doubt Commodore Vanderbilt would rejoice exceedingly if the lawsuits were allowed to drop—he can afford it; but Fisk and Gould seem to think the Erie shareholders, English as well as American, would stand a much better chance of receiving an early dividend if the Commodore would only be conscientious enough to drop the five million, as well as the lawsuit, and the proceedings in the suit instituted for the purpose of forcing him to disgorge, it cannot fail to be exeedingly interesting and instructive to those who have been victimized by Messrs. Raphael & Co. It is passing strange, however, that what was so plainly discernable to all the other enemies of Erie, had to be *pointed out* to the concoctors of the infamous "protection" conspiracy. And the questions naturally arise, what has so suddenly opened the eyes of the men who have hitherto been so lamentably, confessedly, and may be criminally blind to the interests they are now so suspiciously anxious to protect? What assurance have the English shareholders that Messrs. Raphael Heath & Co. will not make use of the extraordinary powers which they so arrogantly assumed for their own enrichment?

It would appear that, notwithstanding their claims to high standing, etc., the members of the Erie Protection Committee are by no means above suspicion. For instance, Messrs. Gould and Fisk claim to be in possession of proofs, furnished by their agent in London, that the members of the so-called Erie Protective Committee are merely agents of a gigantic conspiracy formed by the union of the interests of the New York Central and Pennsylvania Central lines to crush out the Erie as a competing line. The main object of the English clique, it is alleged, is to secure possession of the $50,000,000 of stock now owned on the other side, and, after getting it transferred into their own names, dispose of the proxies to the managers of the two above-named antagonistic corporations, both of which have recently secured the passage of laws authorizing them to purchase. But Gould and Fisk, it will be objected, are very deeply prejudiced against the prime movers of the projection scheme, and are consequently willing to believe anything that may be advanced to their discredit. Well, as this is not at all unlikely, in fact highly probable, it may be well to make all due allowances. In this connection, however, the Erie directors are not the only parties who doubt the sincerity of Raphael & Co's declaration of disinterestedness, and the indignant protest, which was published in the English journals over the signatures of a large number of holders of Erie, deserves most serious consideration.

PROTEST OF FOREIGN SHAREHOLDERS.

The undersigned, holders of a large number of shares of the Erie Railroad Company, do most earnestly protest against the action lately taken by the so-called Erie Protection Committee as being contrary to the true interests of the shareholders. In justification of their protest they beg to state that after the minutest inquiries they have discovered that the demand by the above committee of one shilling per share, and the stamping of it under the menace of it being excluded from the stock market, is nothing but a blind, calculated to coerce the shareholders to dispossess themselves from their most valuable right of electing a new manager of the Erie Railroad Company, without having previously been made acquainted either with the name or the qualifications of the candidate for the management of said company whom the Protection Committee intend to support at the next election. The fact that not less than 400,000 or 500,000 shares can, by such a wholesale registration as advised by the committee in favor of trustees, insure the election of an unknown person as manager of such an important company, without his having to buy, as in ordinary way, the required number of shares which would give him the majority of votes, must be well understood by the shareholders, who would thus lose through such an inconsiderate registration all the benefit of higher prices which their shares would necessarily attain if bought successively by the unknown candidate or his party desirous to obtain the control of the new elections.

We have reason to believe that the well known, influential party who has been for many years trying in New York to get the management of the Erie Company would cheerfully pay a large amount as a bonus to have the 400,000 or 500,000 shares held in this country registered in their name or in those of their friends, in order to conquer for the candidate of their choice the position of the Erie Railroad King. The well-combined, but too transparent plan of the so-called Protection Committee has no other object than to take from the hands of the shareholders, without giving them any compensation whatever, the most valuable right of electing an unknown person as manager of such an important company, and dispensing him and his party from buying the majority of its stock, which, if bought by such a person or party in competition with the party now in power, would raise the price of shares at least fifty dollars.

The above explanation will suffice to prove that somebody else but the shareholders would get the enormous bonus, which may be easily calculated, and which would be gladly paid by the candidate manager proposed and supported by the so-called Protection Committee. Our fellow shareholders will, therefore, do well to abstain from falling into this new trap, by tightly holding their shares, and by refusing to sign any paper whatsoever or to pay any shilling fee or accept any stamping, which ceremonials are but a blind to a scheme which should be denounced for their benefit. It is sincerely hoped that the London press and the board of stockbrokers will immediately discountenance the action and measures lately taken by the pretended Protection Committee, as their maintenance would inaugurate, in the first financial centre of the world, a most disastrous system of organizing similar protection committees, which would spring up like mushrooms along the long list of stocks and which, under the pretence of protection and stamping, would extort shilling fees for registration of shares in favor of such or such opposition party from shareholders already sufficiently bled by exorbitant commissions and by the unscrupulous mismanagement of their companies.

Having read the above, Mr. Crouch continued:

This protest, gentlemen, bears the signatures of the more sensible of the English shareholders, and also the names of many influential American residents. The latter, in their laudable anxiety to sustain American credit abroad, have been mainly instrumental in exposing the designs of the *soidisant* Protection Committee. However foolishly they have acted in other respects, the British stock-jobbers, who are at the head of this new fillibustering raid on the Erie treasury, deserve considerable credit for their more than Yankee smartness in raising the funds necessary for the accomplishment of their private ends. Their first move plainly demonstrated that they are as little inclined to stick at trifles as the more reckless and disreputable of their American allies. Calling a meeting of stockholders in London, the leading conspirators voted themselves into power as a committee, and no sooner were the self-constituted protectors thus empowered than they commenced plucking their poor proteges by the imposition of a tax of one shilling per share. With a view to forcing all holders on the other side to submit to this extortion, and to securing absolute control of the English interest, Raphael & Co. went so far as to threaten that shares not bearing their stamp should be excluded from the London stock market. Why, the Erie Directors have not even been accused of attempting anything half so despotic as this first act of the English protectorate. Protectorate! Heaven save the mark! While anxious to do all that lies in their power to satisfy the just and reasonable demands of the foreign shareholders when properly presented, the Erie Directors are compelled in self-defense, and for the defense of all parties interested, to use all the means at their disposition to frustrate the schemes of the unscrupulous clique of speculators represented by Mr. Burt The fact is, as Mr. Fisk declares, in his figurative but forcible style, these Englishmen—Raphael, Heath & Co.—have gone in on a whirl of speculation; they are all on the make, and are going in for what they can root out. Judging by the vigorous opposition Vanderbilt's English agents have had to contend with on both sides of the Atlantic since the timely exposure of their plans Mr. Fisk was also right when he prophesied that they would not make enough to pay for court plaster to cover the raw spots which the rooting process would inevitably cause on their respective snouts. The language of the irrepressible Admiral may not always be elegant, but it is wonderfully expressive.

BURT'S CLAIMS CONSIDERED.

In the somewhat contradictory statement Mr. Burt made before the Committee, he made the best of a very bad case He claimed to represent $50,000,000 of the entire share capital of the Company; but, as I understand, produced no credentials in support of his preposterous pretentions. The question is how much is Mr. Burt *authorized* to represent? Jay Gould, for instance, owns about 2,000,000 out of the 50,000,000 Mr. Burt claims to represent; but it is hardly likely that the President of the Erie road authorized Raphael & Co. to ask for the repeal of the Directors' bill on his account. Fisk, who is also carrying stock in London, is, I imagine, rather opposed to the scheme of the self-constituted Protection Committee than otherwise. Then, again, the shares of the large body of foreign stockholders, who see through and protest against the selfish schemes of the English conspirators, are to be deducted from Mr. Burt's round total, making it fine by degrees and beautifully less, and causing our faith in the sincerity of all the other claims advanced by him, as the mouthpiece of the three conspirators, from whom he derives the little authority he has, to dwindle in proportion. The amount really represented by the agent of the English ring is a comparatively unimportant point, however. He would be entitled to a hearing if he only represented one share.

Now, then, let us see how far his complaint as made to this Committee is worthy of consideration. In the first place, he says: "Before the election in 1868, the transfer books of the Company were closed for sixty days. The articles of association of the Erie Railway Company provide that no transfers shall be made for ten days next previous to the annual election of Directors. I have not been able to see the by-laws of that Company, and cannot say whether any alteration has been made in those articles of association since 1861; but I am assured that the practice of Companies is to close their transfer books for only thirty days before the election of Directors, while on this occasion the books of the Erie Railway Company were closed for sixty days." The by-laws of which Mr. Burt pretends to have no knowledge, provided that no transfers should be made for thirty days. For his further information it may be stated that the by-laws and articles of association were framed for the express purpose of preventing transfers within the time limited, and of enabling the Company, whenever it may be found necessary, to close the books for a longer time. There has been no uniform practice regulating the time of closing the books before election, and at the period referred to it was necessary to close the books sixty days on account of the enormous amount of transfers, so that the books might be written up. Every Company make its own regulations in this respect.

Secondly. It is complained that "The present Board was elected in 1868, and they were elected for one year, and they would have gone out of office on the second Tuesday in October, 1869, and the shareholders would then have had an opportunity of expressing their opinion." In answer to this, it is simply necessary to state that the Board which Mr. Burt said would have gone out, *did* go out, and that the shareholders, who in that contingency would have had an opportunity, *did* have an opportunity of expressing their opinion, and made the best possible use of it by electing the present Board. The next objection is a very serious one. In criticising the charter of the Erie Railway Company, the English lawyer objects that "the power given to the Directors by the Legislature are far greater than are ever given in such cases in England; and it seems that the only protection which the Erie shareholders have in respect to the conduct of their Directors, is the annual election. They have no right to call any extraordinary special meeting in the course of the year; they have no means of examining the affairs or accounts of the Company, and they are solely at the mercy and discretion of the Directors for the whole year. It is only, therefore, once a year, at the general election, that they have an opportunity of expressing their judgment as to the management and policy of the Directors; and, that being so, I am sure I need not say that it is the most important and valuable right which the shareholders of the Company possessed."

Gentlemen, should you make up your minds to acknowledge the superior wisdom of English legislators, I would then ask you to consider Mr. Burt's complaints as to the large powers granted to American directors, &c., &c., in view of the fact that the English shareholders of Erie have never appeared personally, and but to a small extent by proxy, at the annual meetings of the Company, and then decide whether it may not be justly claimed, considering their apathy heretofore, that the law in question was framed in the interest of these lukewarm English permanent stockholders, and to prevent control of the election by the purchase and sale of the proxies of their speculative compatriots.

Mr. Burt told this Committee he knew of no other case in which any other mode of managing the affairs of a railroad company had been adopted than the election of directors annually.

Had he taken the trouble to make any inquiry on this head, he would have found a number of precedents for the classification adopted by the Erie shareholders. Several other American companies in different States have taken advantage of a law, in every respect similar to the so-called Erie bill, and in classifying their directors have found it for the interest of their roads, that, to use Mr. Burt's own language, 'there shall be *permanence* in the management of railway companies, and that it should not be possible for speculators to get hold of shares, and hold them for a few weeks, long enough to turn out the existing Board of Directors, and substitute another Board, not for the advantage of the public or of the shareholders, but for their own advantage.'

In conclusion, it is evident from Mr. Burt's own showing, that nothing is so likely to defeat the above desirable end, than the very thing for which he so inconsiderately clamors on behalf of his clients—the repeal of the classification bill. Should this wise and beneficial law be annulled, the trials and troubles of Erie will commence anew, the voting power of the majority will be vested in the hands of the three unscrupulous speculators who are behind Mr. Burt, and the permanence of such a management as would be formed by President Raphael, Comptroller Heath, and their English associates, with their legal agent as Treasurer, could only result in the utter ruin of the vast and magnificent property they are so utterly incapable of controlling.

As an English stockholder, therefore, for myself, and in behalf of such of the foreign stockholders as Mr. Burt does *not* represent, I would respectfully ask that this Committee would postpone its decision, and hold over the petition for the repeal of the Erie bill until those of the shareholders on the other side who protest against this pernicious protection scheme, and who ask, through me, to be saved from such friends as Raphael & Co., have had an opportunity of submitting their views."

It now remains to be seen whether the legislators of the Empire State will stultify themselves by repealing a law, which is also the law of the States of Pennsylvania, Ohio, and Illinois, at the insulting request, or rather demand, of three or four London stockjobbers, who are conspiring to obtain control of the Erie Railway—the Broadway of the American continent. This demand is all the more insulting, since, as Mr. Burt himself admits, the more important of the English Railway Corporations are governed by a similar law.

THE BATTLE OF THE BRITISHERS.

Albany Correspondence of the N. Y. Sun, March 31, 1870.

THE ERIE FIGHT.

The battle on the Erie Directors classification bill was resumed to-day before the Assembly Railroad Committee. Burt and Crouch, the representatives of the rival English interests, being the contestants. Neither Mr. Gould nor his counsel were present, the Erie forces having assumed an attitude of armed neutrality. The Anglo-American stockholder first stepped into the arena and replied to the attack made by the British barrister as follows:

" Lawyers are licensed to be abusive, as physicians are licensed to kill. The able counsel for the Erie Railway Company, Mr. Shearman, gave you to understand that there was a difference between what he said as a lawyer and what he said as a man. In consideration of the fact that he is a stranger in the land, I make the same distinction between the statements of Burt and the lawyer and the man. Burt the lawyer told you he could always 'answer the fool according to his folly.' It comes easy to him, I suppose. Being no lawyer I do not consider it worth my while to answer 'the fool' at all, but I will do Mr. Burt the justice to say that I do not consider him a fool by any means, and it must be apparent to the Committee that if there was not something serious and damaging in the protests of the shareholders represented by me, Mr. Burt would not have honored me with the exceedingly flattering attention bestowed yesterday. I congratulate myself however upon the significant fact that Mr. Burt confined himself to criticisms and misquotations from the pamphlet entitled 'A Second Chapter of Erie' and failed to make satisfactory reply to any one of the points of my argument before the Senate Committee. I said I did not consider Mr. Burt a *fool*. If he is as wise as I take him to be, he will do well to cure himself of the peculiar kind of kleptomania with which he is afflicted. By his own confession he is guilty of filching a document which he saw Mr. Gould 'lose' in the Senate Committee room yesterday. He gloried in the theft, and flourished the paper before you."

Mr. Burt here interrupted, and said he protested against the matter being regarded in that light. His opponent continued:

"I have no knowledge of the affair but your own confession, and that confession was made to this Committee. I want no other witnesses than the gentlemen who saw you with the paper in your hand, and heard you tell how you came by it. But, gentlemen, I have another charge of a similar nature to make. Last night a document was missed from this room, and the gentleman who now occupies the chair (the Hon. Mr. Patrick of Chemung) arrested Mr. Burt on suspicion while leaving the room, and on Mr. Burt's capacious pockets being searched it was discovered that he had coolly possessed himself of it. To that document, which had been consigned to the Hon. Eugene Durnin, the clerk of this Committee, our champion of English honesty had no more right than a pickpocket has to his plunder. Gentlemen, there appears to be such a method in Mr. Burt's madness that I consider it my duty to caution such of you as have any papers relating to this Erie business about you to keep a very sharp eye on him." [Loud laughter, in which Mr. Burt did not join].

Mr. Burt was so much embarrassed at the effect of this *expose* that he held over his defence. A special meeting of the Committee is to be held for the purpose of considering such excuses as he may be able to prepare in the meantime. The Chairman and Clerk of the Committee being the principal witnesses against him, however, conviction is almost certain. This kleptomania business has damaged him and his cause to an irretrievable extent. There is serious talk to-night of making this matter a question of privilege of the House.

Mr. Crouch then went over the main points of his statement to the Senate Committee, and delivered a long and able argument, setting forth some strong extenuating circumstances connected with the present management, and making vigorous opposition to the repeal of the classification bill on the petition of the London Erie Protection Committee.

Mr. Burt, after a lame attempt at damaging Mr. Crouch's argument, replied at some length to the eloquent defence put forward by Mr. T. G. Shearman yesterday on behalf of the Erie Railway Company, but it was evident that he spoke as one without hope.

SOL.

THE COMING DIVIDEND.

From the Stenographer's Report.

Mr. Crouch then went on to say:

Gentlemen, I assure you I am as anxious for a dividend as any of Mr. Burt's clients, and so are the holders of the two million dollar's worth of stock, whose interest I am now endeavoring to protect; but we do not join in the inconsiderate clamors of those who have been scared out of their votes by Raphael & Co. It is asked: "If these men are such good managers, why do they not pay dividends?" I say the present managment *have* paid dividends, *are* paying them; large ones too—dividends to the traveling public, and that in paying those dividends first, they have put the earnings of the company to the best possible use—*the only use in fact to which they had any right to put them, considering the dangerous condition of the road.* Had they not spent the enormous sums they have in order to make the road safe, they might have paid dividends to the stockholders. But, while the stockholders were pocketing such dividends, what fearful disasters might not have happened, owing to the shameful condition in which the track, the rolling stock, etc., had been left by the men who paid paltry dividends with the money the road needed so badly, and so pacified the stockholders whom they were plundering, and whose property they were ruining.

The last dividend from the previous management was paid at the price of 28 lives, and the maiming of some 60 passengers, and resulted financially in a loss of two millions of dollars to the company. I refer to the Carr's Rock catastrophe, that frightful illustration of the terrible consequences of forcing dividends at the expense of the road. And, mind you, Gould and Fisk had nothing to do with this, although it is so often cited as an instance of *their* mismanagement. This awful warning to impatient stockholders, occured in the good old dividend-paying days of Gould's predecessor, remember. I advise all dividend-desiring Stockholders, American and foreign, to cease this suicidal interference with the managers of their property. Let Gould and Fisk go on with the work they have so well commenced, and are so admirbly fitted to finish, and larger dividends will be forthcoming than ever before.

THE ERIE BUILDING.

And now, a few words about the removal of the headquarters of the Company from the dirt and confusion of West Street to the elegant and commodious building which adorns the corner of 23d Street and 8th Avenue. Here again the enterprising Erie managers point the way of progress. No one who has given the future of New York a moments thought can doubt that in a very short time the neighborhood in which the principal offices of the great Corporation are now located will be the commercial centre of the city. What if the directors' rooms are handsomely and substantially furnished? What if the employes have pleasant and comfortable surroundings while at work? This is an age of improvement and refinement as well as of invention. Why should Railroad Corporations be behind Banking and Insurance Companies in this respect? Compare the palatial buildings occupied by our leading journals—such as keep pace with the age—with such dingy dens as the Tribune office. Contrast the filthy festoons which the spiders weave from day to day over Mr. Greeley's old white hat, with the artistic tracings which glow upon the lofty ceil of the Herald *sanctum sanctorum*, and you have some idea of the difference between the old and new Erie Buildings. Drew didn't mind cobwebs! He no more thought of removing them than he did the worn-out rails on the Erie road. The new brooms have made a clean sweep of both however. More power to them. (Loud laughter.) All who have visited the Erie Building admit that nothing could be more pleasing or appropriate than the frescoes which adorn this magnificent temple, dedicated to the genius of the iron age. Banners bearing the portraits of Fulton, Franklin, Watts and Morse waive from the four corners of the main ceiling; tablets inscribed respectively: "New York," the initial point, and "Chicago," "St. Louis" and "San Francisco," the principal objective points of the Erie line, fill up the central compartments, and exquisitely executed groups of allegorical figures and trophies of railroad implements and machinery meet the eye at every turn—symbols of the mighty power of the God, Steam—the Jupiter of the mythology of science, who breaths the breath of life as it were into the nostrils of the iron-horse.

The rollicking Ramsey, of Albany and Susquehanna notoriety, circulated some exceedingly amusing fictions based upon the fact that there is a theatre somewhere in rear of the extensive structure on 23d Street. The Grand Opera House however is to the Erie Building what Niblo's theatre is to the Metropolitan Hotel—a separate and distinct establishment. Vanderbilt has a weakness for fast horses, Fisk is a patron of the drama, and Ramsey is one of those dog-in-the-manger sort of people who delight to bark and bite at everybody. Every one to his taste, gentlemen.

Now then, let Mr. Burt make up his mind to avail himself of High Priest Gould's courteous invitation, and when he returns from his trip over the road and enters the portals of the Erie Temple he too will fall down and worship.

THE CLASSIFICATION BILL.

I would ask you to bear in mind that Mr. Burt does not

think there is anything wrong in the bill itself. He admits that some of the principal railroads in England are governed by a law exactly similar in its operation, and admitting that, he acknowledges that he cannot possibly find any fault with it, since in his estimation whatever is English is right. He has discovered that the law you thought fit to adopt had been previously adopted in other States of the Union, and is now in force in Pennsylvania, Ohio, Illinois, Wisconsin and elsewhere, and that here in New York it applies to the Hudson River, Harlem and Central lines as well as to the Erie, and consequently, was *not* framed for the especial benefit of any set of Directors, and yet he deliberately makes the insulting demand that you shall repeal it for the especial benefit of his clients. Who are his clients? Three London stock-jobbers who have obtained a number of shares under false pretences, and who had the audacity to count upon *your* assistance to enable them to lord it over the commerce of the great through-line of the continent, as thanks to their Alabamas, British shipowners now monopolize the carrying trade of the Atlantic.

Gentlemen, I am sure Mr. Burt sees his mistake, and I think he is sorry for it. An Englishman by birth, I feel myself bound to apologise for him. An American by adoption, and in feeling, I ask you as American legislators to reject this foreign petition for the repeal of a law of the sovereign State of New York.

Foreigners may appeal to our Courts, but I maintain that none but citizens of the Republic should have a voice in the making and un-making of our laws.

www.ingramcontent.com/pod-product-compliance
Lightning Source LLC
LaVergne TN
LVHW021403110826
845150LV00007B/1759

* 9 7 8 1 4 2 5 5 1 2 3 1 6 *